MW00474117

The Big Three Let Me Reach 93

The Good Lord, A Guardian Angel, And Dumb Luck

by Robert W. "Bob" Schottelkorb

as told to Lindsay Combs

The Big Three Let Me Reach 93
The Good Lord, A Guardian Angel, And Dumb Luck

Copyright © 2015 by Robert Warren Schottelkorb

Transcribed and edited by Lindsay Combs
Cover design by Lindsay Combs

ISBN-13: 978-1517366803
ISBN-10: 1517366801

All rights reserved. No part of this book may be reproduced or transmitted in any form or by any means, electronic or mechanical, including photocopying, recording, or by any information storage and retrieval system without the written permission of the author, except in the case of brief quotations embodied in critical articles and reviews.

Table of Contents

Acknowledgements…………………………………………………………………5

Part 1: Growing Up………………………………………………………………7

Part 2: Mexico………………………………………………………………...43

Part 3: Training………………………………………………………………77

Part 4: Overseas…………………………………………………………...115

Part 5: Life After the War…………………………………………………...171

Acknowledgements

Little did I dream that when I took my granddaughter Lindsay at nine months old for a walk in the light rain to help her stop crying that 25 years later she would help me get all my ramblings down into a book. Thank you, Lindsay!

Part 1:
Growing up

At Seeley Lake with Ken Rigby – Summer 1936 after graduation from grade school
When I had my elbow cocked that meant, 'I may be small, but don't underestimate me!'

My name is Robert Warren Schottelkorb. That's a bit of a mouthful so it's just Bob, and this is my story. I don't want it too bland, who cares about when I was born and such. But I do want to thank my mom and dad for choosing such an ideal place to be born and raised in as Missoula, Montana. Located 500 miles east of Seattle, Washington and about 200 miles south of the Canadian border, Missoula is nestled in a valley surrounded by steep hills and snow-covered peaks. With the natural beauty of the mountains, rivers, and the wildlife, it was a beautiful place to live and grow up in. Missoula's elevation is about 3,200 feet and the climate is quite pleasant most of the year thanks to the Continental Divide to the east keeping the weather moderate. The Pacific Coast rain mostly falls west of the mountains and leaves Missoula close to semi-arid with rainfall reaching fourteen inches or so a year, meaning we have to water our lawns and irrigate crops. The Blackfoot River, a beautiful river known for recreation and fishing, flows into the Clark Fork River just east of Missoula. The Clark Fork cuts across the valley through town and is a tributary of the Columbia River, which empties into the Pacific Ocean. As it gets further west past town, the Bitterroot River joins the Clark Fork and has its headwaters on the northern slopes of the Continental Divide. It is the border between Montana and Idaho, over 100 miles south of Missoula.

Showing off all four seasons, the temperature can get up to 100°F in the summer and, although the winters have become milder in recent years, it could get as low as 40 below 0°F. The snow has historically been around 42 inches or so per year but it is subject to the ever-changing thawing and melting cycles. Missoula is influenced by Pacific coastal weather, whereas east of the Continental Divide, roughly two thirds of the rest of Montana, it is very open and subject to strong winds and the weather from Canada. The central and eastern parts of the state enjoy more sunlight but also more widely varying temperatures than the mountainous western third. They might experience a warm Chinook spring wind in the winter with melting snow only to have it suddenly halted in a flurry of snow and blizzard conditions. Both eastern and western Montana have their own special beauty.

Where I was raised thrived a sheltered mix of pine and fir forests and grassy valleys. By this time, the 1920s and 30s, the population of Missoula was around 13,000 and was growing slowly. My folks had bought a house in town and it was quite nice, but it just had two bedrooms. My older brother Bill and I shared a double bed in our room and we seemed to get along fine. We didn't have much of a problem with it because that's the way it had to be. Our house had a large living room, which had plenty of room for formal dining, when company was present, a good-sized kitchen, and a little breakfast nook with a westward-facing window. The window was a bit too small for our liking, but you could look out into the garden area and beyond all the same.

Mom and Dad were both the eldest in their families, so they grew up with more responsibility and helped raise their younger siblings, which reflected in their personalities. My mom, Eva Loraine Hooper, was born in Springfield, Missouri on October 25th, 1892. They traveled to the Bitterroot Valley near Stevensville, Montana when she was a young girl around ten or twelve years old. I wish I had asked her more questions about her younger years, especially since they had traveled by covered wagon. I can't imagine how that had been. What had the journey been like? Had they been pulled by oxen, mules or horses? But she had never said much about it, and I had never thought to ask.

Dad was William John Schottelkorb, born October 28th, 1887. His parents both came from Germany. My grandfather had been a coal miner in Bavaria and he and his brother each married two sisters from Germany when they arrived here. When World War I was on, some people questioned the Germans about loyalty, but my grandfather took the attitude that his new country was just like having a new bride. If the mother country tried to interfere and tell him what to do he would say, hold on now mother, I'm an American now and this is my home and my new life.

My grandfather was gentle, quiet-spoken, not too tall and rather slender, but he was respected in Missoula, where he worked as a ditch rider, someone who patrolled the irrigation ditches and saw that everybody got their fair share of water. His family moved around a lot before that. First they lived in Corning, Ohio, where my dad was born, then they journeyed down to Texas, and then over to the mines in West Virginia before moving to Butte, Montana, well known for copper and silver mining. As a young man Dad came with his family to finally settle in Missoula. It must have been a tremendous joy that his folks shared to be able to buy their own land of about five acres a few miles south of Missoula. My dad helped his father build a square two-story home on the property, just east of where the road separates upper and lower Miller Creek. Together with his three sisters and two brothers they filled the new house right up. An orchard of apple trees and other fruit trees was planted, and my grandfather also had a truck garden and would peddle fresh fruit and vegetables into nearby Missoula with a horse and buggy.

In the early 1900s Mom worked in Stevensville, just 30 miles south of Missoula, as a telephone switchboard operator. They had a big window facing the main street. Dad was a young mechanic at a garage nearby at the time and he happened to walk by her window one day. Mom said to herself, that's the guy for me, I wouldn't mind marrying him!

Needless to say she had her eyes set on him early on. She knew what she wanted and they were married in 1917. My mom was five years younger than my dad, and I was born on her birthday when she turned 30 on October 25th, 1922. We were a family of October birthdays except for my older brother Bill, William Franklin Schottelkorb, who was born August 30, 1918.

My brother Billy (three years old) with Mom and the Model T
Ready to go on a camping trip

Brother Bill (nearly six) and me (two)

The four of us lived in a comfortable neighborhood less than two blocks from Missoula County High School and half a block away from the Eddy Bakery. There was a nice aroma of freshly baked bread that floated over into our neighborhood. This was at a time not long after the Salish Indians had their tipis along the Clark Fork River. They would occasionally come to the Eddy Bakery and pick up a quantity of bread or sweets.

The Salish Indians were moved from their homeland in the Bitterroot Valley in 1891, when Chief Charlo of the Salish tribe led their own Trail of Tears north to the Flathead Indian Reservation. It was a severe blow to be uprooted from their native land. The Salish still came to the Missoula area to search for the beautiful bitterroot flower. The bulb of the root would be dug up and utilized in their medicines and even added to dried buffalo jerky. They knew the value of the natural flowers and would also gather arrowleaf balsamroot around the hills of Missoula. It had a starchy root and was used as a kind of flour when ground up.

We didn't have much contact with them, but I particularly remember one time when I was around six years old sitting out in the backyard with my dad. A Salish man, who probably had some stature in the tribe, drove by in a one-horse buggy. He was dressed nicely with a tall, black stovepipe hat. Sitting beside him was a Salish woman, presumably his wife.

She had a blanket wrapped around her and as they drove past our backyard in the alley my dad spoke up and said to her, "Well hello, Mary!" and she smiled broadly.

The man looked straight ahead but she did not act offended, my dad simply had his own sense of humor and wanted to greet them. I watched them thoughtfully as they drove silently by.

My world at first was centered around the close neighborhood, as there were four or five other kids about my age. I had quite an imagination and was taken with the game 'let's pretend', and because of that I gradually assumed the unofficial position of the leader of our little group, such as it was. I made up stories to tell and we played them out in a dirt pile in the vacant lot not far from home, turning that dirt pile and vacant lot into anything but.

One of the earliest kids I met was Billy Wood. He lived on Plymouth Street, one block east of Blaine Street, where I lived. When we were both around five years old I was in the back yard acting out one of my stories with Billy, during which he picked up a heavy-duty yard pick lying in the garden while I was coming up behind him. Facing away from me he swung it high over his head in an arc and it caught me just by my face. The pick struck my nose hard and blood immediately gushed out. Billy swung around, took one look at me, I was a bleeding mess, and he ran home panicked and horrified. I ran indoors as well, in my own shock. My mom managed to get me all cleaned up, but she was very upset by the incident. That afternoon she took me by the arm and marched me over to see Mrs. Wood and Billy. She demanded to know why Billy had acted the way he did, but I said I didn't blame him and that it was my fault. Eventually my mom simmered down and we went back home and resumed life.

I did tend to be a bit accident-prone. When I was about two years old I was out in the garage with my dad when he was getting ready to go to work. He was a Ford mechanic and we owned a Ford Model T touring car. The garage door was open and I was in the corner of the garage back beside the car. Dad started engine but he didn't move the car for a bit and the gears started turning in my mind. Since he hadn't moved yet, I thought I definitely had enough time to go to the other side of the car. For some reason getting to the other side was a top priority in my small mind. Just as I started darting across, Dad abruptly backed up, knocked me down, and ran over one of my legs. I yelled and he immediately jumped out of the car and took me in his arms. He checked me over, though there didn't seem to be any damage. The air inflated tires hadn't bothered me at all. Fortunately, I came out of it with hardly a scratch. Dad was only just starting to learn that he had a child who needed a lot of supervision.

Only a year or so later we took the family in the Model T up to Lolo Hot Springs, about 40 miles southwest of Missoula. There were two pools: one directly from the hot springs that didn't have the blend of cold water to make it very swimmable, and a comfortable, larger pool that did. The resort had dressing rooms on the south end of the building, and Mom was heading that way, ready to leave. Sitting me down beside the steps leading into the main pool, she told Dad to watch me while she went in to change back into her street clothes. However, Dad decided he had time to take my older brother Bill for one last little swim on his back into the deep end and he proceeded to do that, leaving me to watch them swim away. I was in a much shallower area of the pool and the water only came up to my legs a little ways. Watching them swim away, I figured that if I took one step down I'd be in deeper water and that would be better, since Bill and Dad were in deeper water as well. Even then I wanted to be like my brother Bill. But, being only three years old, I underestimated the size of the step and the water was instantly over my head. Dad looked back in my direction and saw only bubbles where I had just been. Nobody else was in the immediate vicinity, and he swam as fast as he could to get to me. He pulled me out of the water and took me out into the yard. All I remember is waking up coughing, sputtering and spitting out water while lying on the ground in front of the pool area. Mom hadn't yet returned but I can imagine her horror when she came out and saw me lying on the ground. Dad didn't have to be scolded much by her because it must have scared him to death for a few minutes there as well. It goes without saying that I was somebody who needed to be watched over closely in those early times.

Despite my occasional dance with death, I continued to explore my little world and loved playing with my friends. Billy Wood and I still got together some, but another neighbor kid who lived one block east of my street was Warren Heyer. He was a bit younger than I was, but he was one of the gang. Apparently he had given favorable reports on me to his family and sometimes his mother invited me to stay overnight with Warren, as he was an only child. He was the only one I ever did this with as a child, but I couldn't reciprocate it because of sharing a double bed with my brother Bill. In the morning after a sleepover at Warren's we would all eat breakfast together with his parents and their dog Tippy. One time Mrs. Heyer gave me a bowl of oatmeal, or mush as we commonly termed it, and although it was tasty, it was more than I could eat.

Looking down at the rest in my bowl, I piped up and said, "Boy, Tippy would be insulted to eat this…" and everybody stopped eating and started at me.

There was a brief, yet icy silence.

Thankfully I then hurriedly finished my sentence and said, "…after I got through making a mess of it."

It was as if a rush of air had been let of out of the room. Everything was fine then, but I certainly defined the meaning of a dramatic pause in that moment. I'm not sure why I paused at all, perhaps to swallow a remaining portion of oatmeal or to take a breath, but it had quite the effect.

During one other occasion, when Warren and I had gone to bed, Mrs. Heyer wanted to check on us to see if we were behaving and going to sleep. However, she couldn't get the door open right away and thought we had locked it and were being troublesome.

"Open this door right now, boys!" she said crossly.

Confused, we hollered back, "We didn't do anything!"

After a bit more squabbling she figured out what had happened. It turned out we were having a minor earthquake and the house was feeling the effects of it. Centered near Helena a little over 100 miles to the east, the quake wasn't very strong and we hardly noticed it at all, but it had managed to briefly alter the door frame enough to get the door stuck. Later we found out that Helena had suffered some rather severe damage. A large old time hot spring resort suffered some devastating cracks and was never used again. It was a shame to lose that iconic treasure, though at the time I was more worried about not being thrown out of Warren's house.

After those instances, Warren's family still felt that I was ok to hang out with and I would occasionally go out to where Warren's uncle had a ranch near Helena. Although we were too small to be of any help, we got to sit on the sidelines and watch the branding of cattle and all that goes on with a western ranch, which was all quite fascinating to observe with our young eyes.

As first grade came around I encountered a major crisis. I was set to start at the new Paxson School and I was bawling pretty hard because I didn't want to go to the new school. I wanted to go to the old Roosevelt school where my brother Bill went. No one managed to tell to me that my brother would actually also be attending the new school, but since it never got explained to me I started out first grade with bad feelings. Another discomfort was that most of my friends were slightly younger and weren't starting school until the next year. This left me in a lurch because I had lost my gang, at least during school hours, which left me feeling pretty lonely. The only person I started first grade with was Billy Wood, and shortly afterwards he and his family moved to a different area and he went to the Roosevelt school. All in all it would have been better if I had been held back a year, but Mom was so proud of me and thought I'd do just fine, so I started earlier. It was a handicap because I was still discovering the world around me and I just wanted to play. I didn't want to be a student. I was also the smallest boy in my class throughout grade school. However, my classmates respected me and I was never bullied.

Paxson Elementary School was only about four blocks from where I lived, but to get there I passed by many open lots with no houses. When the spring flowers were out I often stopped to admire and sometimes pick them. My obligation to go to school forced me to move along, but I developed an early love for hiking and nature, including the wildflowers: first the buttercups, then bluebells, yellow bells, and Johnny jump-ups. There were also a few scattered bitterroots, but not too many right close down in the valley.

I also developed an early love for nature and hiking, partially thanks to my brother. In grade school he and his friend Ed Halm took me up Pattee canyon, a beautiful hiking area in the hills a few miles to the southeast of Missoula. We camped overnight, but I was not the best companion for them because I was still pretty young and Ed was only tolerant of me. He wouldn't have been tolerant at all except for my brother. Ed thought a lot of Bill, and Bill wanted to get me some shared camping experience. So in the evening, after we were all set up with a campfire and everything, we made dinner. Ed had a frying pan and he made hamburgers. The next morning there wasn't much to eat, and my portion was a leftover hamburger. Cold and not very flavorful, it was kind of the pits. I didn't have a big appetite, but it seemed like we were on the verge of starvation. They set the burger on a log by the little creek we had camped next to and a frog jumped up right next to it.

"Oh!" I cried out in disappointment. I could feel the annoyance from Ed.

Bill simply said, "It didn't touch it, Bob. Go on and eat it."

They were in high school and I was only a fifth grader. Grudgingly I accepted my brother's request and ate the burger, thus introducing me to the wild ways of camping.

I thought Bill was kind of a bossy brother, always telling me what to do. I wanted to be independent, but I realized later it was all for my own good. One time he put together some used bicycle parts and made a smaller bike just for me, his little brother. He used a 26" diameter wheel instead of a 28" diameter standard size so that it would fit me. Then, of course, I had to learn how to ride a bike so he and Ed took me out to Greenough Park to teach me how to ride. It was around Christmas and was very slippery and icy out. Time and time again I kept falling and crying. But with Bill's encouragement, or perhaps his raw determination, I got up and repeated it and that went on for quite a while before he called it quits and we could go home. He always had a big influence on me, and I looked up to him, even if I didn't want to admit it.

Me, eight years old, and my brother Billy, twelve

When Bob and Ted Delaney moved into the neighborhood, well gee, that was something for all of us. Ted was slightly older and Bob was a little younger than me. My brother Bill didn't have too many friends for a while there in his later grade school and he occasionally hung around with us or us with him. One thing we all did together was go to the corner of University Avenue and South Higgins, not far from our homes, and count the Fords and Chevrolets that went by. Bill was a Ford man since our dad was a Ford mechanic, and Bill knew some mechanical trade and was interested in it. While we counted he preached the virtues of Ford over Chevy. Around that time Chevrolet came out with a six-cylinder engine and Ford only had a four-cylinder, but even before that Ford was losing ground until they produced the Model A in 1928. Nevertheless, the count was always pretty close. The Delaneys were a little better off than some of our other friends' parents and they purchased a six-cylinder Chevrolet, which was quite fancy. Cars were pretty important and each year the new Ford models came out in September for the following year. In 1932, when I was around ten, the first Ford with a V8 engine came out and wow, the excitement just kept coming. It had an 85 horsepower engine whereas the Model A was only at 40 horsepower. Every year we all went down and marveled at the latest Fords with their shiny fenders and cool new styles. That was quite an event, with refreshments included.

Our family of four did quite a lot of activities together and also ventured out to visit the extended family from time to time. My mother's grandparents had a nice house in Stevensville. There was no basement or second floor, but it had a comfortable living room with a black stove trimmed with a shiny chrome door and handle where you could add more wood or coal as the case may be. That seemed to keep that area of the house at a reasonable temperature. In the dining room there was a large table with several chairs. On the table there were always a few cut glass dishes with glass lids containing various goodies including fruits, pickled crab apples, sweet watermelon pickles, and all sorts of jams and jellies, which we loved to indulge in. Of course, there were no refrigerators at that time and they pumped water with a hand pump from a well just near the back porch. Their yard was good-sized, great for running around in, with quite a few apple, cherry and other fruit trees. The flag was always up at the flagpole because my great-grandfather was a Union Civil War veteran, and as a very young man in the 1860s he had carried the flag as his duty.

A bunk house was located out in the back and was where Bill and I stayed when we slept over. In the winter it was quite cold, but the bed was stuffed with huge amounts of soft feathers and we'd sink way down. Then the quilt on top of us was a feather quilt and the pillows were filled with feathers also. So keeping warm was no problem and it was very cozy. The little outhouse was less pleasant and was right nearby. Often it was the case that papers and magazines would substitute for toilet paper, so we didn't like to spend any time in there. There was a bucket in the bunk house that we could utilize if we had to pee during the night, which, for us, was more bearable than the smelly outhouse.

Mom certainly enjoyed being around her family, but when we weren't visiting relatives we also had fun taking the Model T on camping trips on the weekends or holidays. Typically our destinations were places with lots of fishing or hot springs, and we didn't have to go far. Mom especially loved to fish and cook and we always had good food, which furthered my joy of camping. Other times, especially over near Lolo Pass into Idaho, we would stop along the way and pick huckleberries, which were used to make yummy pies and jams. Quite often on our trips we were joined by other families such as the Halm family. Our family had become acquainted through Bill's friendship with their son Ed. They also had a younger son named Glenn, and although he was still a good few years younger than me, we also got to be friends with time.

For the most part these journeys were joyful and fun, but there were a few unfortunate ones as well. The scariest trips were when we headed high up on the narrow mountain roads, especially into the Skalkaho divide in the Sapphire Mountains south of Missoula. It was a very steep grade in places and was just a dusty dirt road. In some areas it was so steep that the Model T couldn't make it and would stall. High up there on the edge of the mountainside I would start crying, it was very scary. All of us except Dad, who had to drive, got out and pushed. This included me and even my mom as well who, later in life, was also very scared of high narrow roads, probably thanks to our traumatic experiences on these trips up the divide. With us pushing the car it lightened the load enough so that we could always continue on, but I don't remember those occasions with particularly happy feelings.

On one other occasion, just before I entered the fourth grade and was about nine years old, we were camping overnight at Rock Creek about 25 miles east of Missoula. We camped next to a nice stream and were having a pleasant time until I started getting stomach pains. Soon it started to hurt so badly that Dad decided to try and ease my pain by heating some rocks in the fire ring and putting one or two wrapped in a towel over my abdomen. That seemed to help a little bit, but it was continuing and we left earlier than planned that day because of my condition. After we arrived in Missoula, we called the doctor and he came out to our house. He was pretty sure I had appendicitis and said that I should be taken to the hospital without further delay.

Upset, I appealed to dad and said, "Please Dad, don't let them do it!"

I could see he was considering that option but mom immediately interjected.

"You can't let a child tell you how to make a decision like that," she said firmly.

Mom's opinion carried and I was entered in the hospital. It wasn't too long before the three doctors at the hospital all came in the room and looked me over. They decided that an operation for appendicitis was indeed what I needed, and I was wheeled away into the operating room. Afterwards the doctor mentioned that my appendix was very badly swollen and infected and that putting the hot rocks on it was exactly the wrong thing to do because it could have encouraged the rupture of the appendix and spread deadly bacteria into the body cavity, so we were fortunate that didn't occur, and once again I got through another risky situation.

For the most part our family vacations with the Model T were very enjoyable and again make me thankful that I grew up in a beautiful place like Montana. We didn't have TV then, of course, or much else to play with in the house, so our entertainment was the great outdoors.

When I was getting ready to start eighth grade a new family moved into the neighborhood and bought the little grocery store about two blocks away from our house. They were the Rigby's. The family consisted of two brothers, a mom and dad, and a grandmother and grandfather. The grandfather was pretty elderly and a large man in not too good of health. The grandmother was a small woman, but quite wiry and alert. Mr. Rigby was a very intelligent man with an electrical background who worked as a safety engineer with a Montana power company and Mrs. Rigby was quite a go-getter and an ambitious woman. They had two boys: Jack, the oldest, and Ken, who also happened to be entering eighth grade.

Ken was a little bit older than me, but I barely came to his shoulder. I was still growing as an eighth grader and even going into high school I was always behind the others. Ken had achieved his growth and was about 5'10" or close to it. He had a deep voice and was fully developed, you might say, and I was still a kid. But we hit it off right away and I asked him why he was attracted to me as a friend. He said it was because I was the leader of the little gang of friends. I couldn't argue with that reasoning, but I still tried to make up for the difference by being pretty spunky. Wanting to prove that I was a tough little guy, from time to time we battled quite vigorously with branches or long sticks and I would try to hold my own. I about gave him all he wanted as a worthy opponent, or so it seemed.

His arrival in town was quite a change in my life and he and I became best friends. I began to fade away from my neighborhood friends, though we did do some things together every now and then. I started getting interested in some of Ken's interests, especially when it came to guns. Ken was a gun nut and soon I adapted that attitude too and we often talked guns or went out to shoot gophers (ground squirrels) in an area west of town called Frenchtown Valley in our spare time. We weren't too serious about it, but it provided an outlet for us to shoot at things.

Another interest we shared was biking. One time we took our bicycles and headed out to camp overnight up at Pattee Canyon, like I had done with Bill and Ed a few years before. Pattee Canyon has a fairly steep incline, only a few miles, but it seemed like a long way when we were pushing our bikes up with our camping gear. Of course, our bikes didn't have any gears like the modern ones now. Huffing and puffing, we finally reached the top of the ridge and could then continue riding. As the elevation leveled off, we came to a good picnic area with lots of tall, shady pine and fir trees. There was a little stream there called Deer Creek that flowed down into the eastern part of Missoula. We dropped down next to the creek and found a prime camping place, a small clearing not too steep and not too close to the water itself. With only a few fences it was an open area, either owned by the Forest Service or state owned, though we never came across any trouble with land ownership.

Before making the trip, Ken, ever fateful to his ideas of the way things should be done, which was in a manly and western way, didn't approve of me wanting to take some bags of tea along. I hadn't developed a taste for coffee like he had. Wandering around in the drug store we finally came across something that could work as a compromise.

"It wouldn't be too civilized if I had sassafras tea, would it?" Ken noted contemplatively. "So let's bring that."

Sassafras has a strong distinctive flavor and didn't seem nearly as dainty as normal tea. At the campsite we boiled the little pieces of the root bark we had purchased at the drug store and concocted a manly enough drink to satisfy Ken's desire for being a real western cowboy.

As night fell we were feeling pretty pleased with ourselves. Our little campfire was crackling softly in the cool night air and the bubbling of the creek was soothing. We were sitting in comfortable silence when I heard something.

"Did you hear that?" I asked suddenly, sitting up straight.

Ken's eyes met mine and they said that he had. It was the sound of twigs snapping and something scratching against bark, and it seemed to be above us.

"What if it's a mountain lion or something?" he asked nervously.

We both peered into the trees. We could see nothing, only a few stars peeping through the darkness of the trees.

"Just keep the fire going," I said, hurriedly throwing some more wood onto our small campfire. Ken started gathering more wood as well. We sat around that campfire and kept it going all through the night, trying not to think too much about what lurked beyond its protective rays of light. When the sun finally came up we were both feeling pretty groggy, but certainly glad that we hadn't been eaten or chewed on.

Never knowing what exactly we had heard that night, the next time we camped we decided to carry a small saw and axe out of precaution. We also decided to build a lean-to. This entailed using dead lodgepole pine branches and wiring them to two trees thick enough to support their weight. We didn't want an animal to sneak up behind us. Essentially, we made a shelter like a cage with a smaller opening at the front to enter, and we sure slept better after that.

Even though we enjoyed biking and camping, Ken and I wanted to get wheels. Ken had spotted this old Willys Whippet Sedan that was offered at 50 dollars and he approached me with the idea of buying it together, though we were both pretty tight on money. I was under the impression that if you bought something like a gun or camping equipment it wasn't wasting money because you had something to show for it, which was better than blowing it away on something like candy or beer. So I paid my 25 dollars, since a car was undoubtedly something to show for, although I never told my folks about it. There was no insurance or anything like that to worry about, so it was all ours and Ken kept it at his place. The Whippet, however, was a strictly uncool car, but it was a start.

With the help of his folks, Ken later managed to buy an older, used Ford Model A roadster. It didn't come with much, there was no top for instance, but it was definitely a big improvement, at least in the cool factor, to the old Willys, and he was proud of his purchase. On one particular occasion Ken probably regretted that his new car had no top when he and I went to see the new King Kong movie. We were in high school and it was a beautiful October night with moonlight. We exited the theater in awe. The movie had impressed us. This King Kong gorilla had jumped over skyscrapers and everything! All of the action still very present in our minds, we parted ways and Ken headed over to his Model A. Just as he started to pull away, thinking he was safe and heading home for the night, I felt a sudden inspiration and sprinted after him. Light on my feet, I jumped on the back of the bumper, learned over the back of the car and grabbed him around the throat, giving him a pretty good squeeze. He immediately slumped down. The car went over to the curb and slowed, drifting past where he had meant to turn. Then the car coasted to a stop.

"Ken? Did I get you?" I asked innocently. A long pause followed.

Then Ken turned around. "Bob," he started, "never do that again. I about had a heart attack!"

"Why didn't you do something?" I asked Ken, laughing as I sat up.

He threw his hands in the air. "I don't know, I figured it was King Kong the gorilla and he had me and there was no use fighting him!"

I shook my head and laughed again. He had just wilted like a flower. Ken was quite strong and could have given me a pretty good throw for sure, but I had given him a good shock. It had been a mean trick, but I couldn't resist.

As we continued on through high school, one of my old neighborhood friends, George Keeting, and a couple others occasionally joined Ken and me after school. George lived in a large two story house. His dad was manager of the local sugar beet company that produced the commercial sugar supply, so they were a more affluent family. At George's house we liked to play card games like twenty-one and poker, though more often than not we gathered at Ken's family's store. It became a collecting place for the kids, the group. It was a big open store on the ground level and two thirds of the area was the store itself and the other third on the south end held the living quarters, where Ken's grandparents stayed. The rest of the family lived downstairs underneath the store. It was a real dark area, they didn't have many window wells, and the ones they had all faced the back side of the store because the front was the sidewalk along the main street. The place was also a bit dangerous, as there was only one outside entrance at the end of some concrete steps. Above the stairs, on ground level, was a small sloping roof where we all often gathered to talk and hang out. I never went downstairs and I never d about it, but it always gave me an eerie feeling. Ken's family was in that location only about a year and a half. After they sold the store they moved to Daly Avenue close to the university, but in our early high school years the store was the place to meet.

Another friend of mine at the time was Ernie Mitch. He was into big game hunting and one time he suggested we go hunting for deer or even elk in November of 1939. It was hunting season. I was a senior in high school and hadn't done any big game hunting at all, my dad and brother didn't do any, and I hadn't either. We wanted to go to Holland Lake about 80 miles northeast of Missoula. It was a very scenic lake and there was a good forest service trail that led up into the woods. On that day there were several inches of snow on the ground and we weren't very well equipped for it. We didn't have sleeping bags, so between the two of us we carried a tarp that we could fold part-way under us and then over us in case of snow or rain. In addition to that we had just a few blankets because it was cold. We had the idea it was to be a short trip and had a very light food supply. I carried my little 30-30 rifle and had never killed anything with it. Ernie was more experienced, but after we didn't see any tracks of big game we decided to call it a day and we turned around mid-afternoon to start heading back toward the trailhead. It took us longer than we thought, however, and dusk was fast approaching. We realized that unless we could get a fire going we were going to have to make a cold camp overnight. This didn't sound too appealing so we kept hiking and hiking. Soon our light was almost completely gone and it began to sprinkle a cold rain, which didn't add to our morale. We weren't going to make it much further before needing to make some sort of camp.

Surprisingly, lo and behold, in the middle of the woods, we encountered a camp where two middle-aged men had just put up their hunting camp. They turned out to be ranchers from Rainy Lake, north of Seeley Lake, and they had a very large tent. One had his wife along as well and they saw how poorly equipped we were and felt sorry for us. To our joy they invited us to stay overnight with them in their nice tent. We sure didn't hesitate to accept that! They had a large wall-tent about twelve by sixteen feet with room to put our bedding in a corner in the back. There was a warm stove toward one side of the front and dinner was almost ready. They fed us supper, it was good and tasty, and in the morning we also enjoyed a hearty breakfast of fried eggs, bacon and hash brown potatoes. We were two happy kids on our hike back to the car, the ranchers had really saved our bacon, so to speak, and I was still running high on dumb luck.

In high school I made the mistake of never finding what I wanted to do as a career. The so-called counselor was in name only, really, and so I just followed some of the things that Ken wanted to study. He had medical problems and had been interested in being a doctor, and because of that he took a lot of science courses and I simply followed along with him. My brother had taken more practical classes like bookkeeping and typing, but unfortunately I didn't bother with such subjects. I never outgrew the fact that I was not as mature or serious in some ways as the others, always one of the youngest and smallest, and I used that excuse not to settle on my studies as much as I should have.

One thing that also affected my school work was taking on a paper route. My friend Ted Delaney had gotten a route in grade school for a relatively short time and I felt that was a good way to earn money. He'd have to get up at about four o'clock and take his bicycle across the river to the newspaper headquarters and pick up the local paper, The Daily Missoulian. Ted had Route 21 on the south side of Missoula. It was ten miles in length and spread out over quite a bit of the southern outskirts of town. Ted had had enough of it after only a short while, but for me, the lure of the money was what drew me in and I took over his route in eighth grade. I probably should have tried to get a more compact route because it was a tough one and took a long time to complete, but I stayed with it through all four years of high school.

The paper route was especially a chore in the winter. One March the snow was still on the ground, thick and damp. Unfortunately, I had a bike where snow built up quickly between the fenders and the tires and locked it in place. On this particular March morning I was so tired and worn out I had to stop and cry when my bike got stuck. Although I was only a few blocks away from home I wondered how I was going to get my bike all the way there. I didn't have anything with me such as a little stick to try and clear out the fender, but somehow I managed to pull it along. Fully exhausted and distressed I didn't bother going to what remained of school that day.

The only blessing on my route was Shep, a Shepherd Collie dog I had gotten from Ken. Mom wasn't too keen on him at first. She was raised as a farm girl and said dogs belonged outside. But Bill and I made such a fuss over Shep that he was eventually let in the house and he slowly adopted himself into our family. He accompanied me all the time on my route. Sometimes if sleep overcame me I'd stand with my feet on each side of the bike and put my head on the handlebars for about five or ten minutes. Shep sat patiently beside me until I roused myself and continued on. One morning there was a cold, miserable rain coming down and Shep was on the porch. He looked at me with a face that said he certainly didn't want to go out into that cold rain.

"You get down here in the rain," I told him, already soaked through. "If I gotta go, then you gotta go."

Loyal as ever, he followed me out into the street. When I got a little older dad let me drive the car on Sunday with the heavy papers, or if the weather was bad enough I got to drive down to the Missoulian to pick up the papers and dear old Shep got to sit in the back seat. He also found the car to be a vast improvement.

The paper route came to be just a part of life. It did have some benefits, as it gave me spending money. I liked to buy revolvers or camping gear or other such goods. Looking back, I think I made around fifteen dollars a week. Around this time Mom's sister, my Aunt Georgia was struggling. She had lost her husband a few years before. He had taken a horse-pulled wagon to a nearby open-pit

With my buddy Shep

coal mine near the surface of the ground and was shoveling coal underneath a part of the mine when it collapsed and killed him. It was a terrible blow to Georgia. She had now remarried, but times were tough, it was during the depression years in the 30s and they had a little farm in eastern Montana south of Laurel. Unfortunately in addition to the depressed prices they had droughts and grasshopper invasions and money was hard to come by. Mom told me about her sad condition and that she needed some financial help. Thanks to my paper route I had a small amount in the bank and my folks didn't have the money to loan her anything so I ended up loaning her about 120 dollars or so. It was amazing that my little paper route, especially in such times, was able to supply some much needed cash.

A year and a half or so later I complained a little to mom that I would like to get my loan repaid. By this time I learned that Georgia and her husband had thrown in the towel and gotten a divorce. It was just too much to endure and they gave it up. Georgia then worked as a cook on a dude ranch in Wyoming, and after a few years she moved to San Francisco and was like a nanny to her older sister Pat's two little girls. So her income became quite sufficient and she could make enough money to enjoy the benefits while living with Pat and her family. Incidentally my loan was paid off years earlier.

During the first part of high school I also worked at Missoula Mercantile, a general store that Bill also worked at. Both Bill and I did janitorial work. He had the night watchman shift and I got the job through him, later becoming a night watchman myself when I was older. At this time in his young life Bill was also rather crazy about the movies, or shows as we called them in that time. He and his friends often got together and sat through two double features. When he had the night watchman job he had to report for his shift about 11:00 or 11:30, but sometimes he went to a show anyway and went straight from there to the job.

Finding time to sleep didn't seem to be a problem for Bill despite his night job and active lifestyle with friends, but I unfortunately had the bad habit of not going to bed early, which didn't pair well with me also having to wake up early for the paper route. Perhaps my parents should have been stricter with me about getting to bed on time, but the situation was that I tended to be short on sleep during the school year. In general I wanted to get up and get it over with, but it was never as simple as that and took quite a while to finish. Because I was often sleep deprived, my solution was study hall. When that hour of the day came around I immediately laid my head down and took a nap and nobody bothered me. The teacher overseeing the study hall didn't complain and kids seemed to leave me alone. I should have been using it to study, of course, but the small nap did help refresh me. I had enough intelligence that I could get by most of the time without studying, and when tests came around I crammed as much as I could. I lived close to the school and as more time went by I started to followed a pattern of carrying home two or three books with the intent of studying after supper, forgetting to study, and then dragging them back the next day unopened. So eventually my grades did start to suffer.

Ultimately it came to the point that if I didn't start doing better in school I wouldn't graduate with my class. It was a bit of a wakeup call, so in order to apply myself I started attending after-class review sessions. But, still a teenager, moments of immaturity were still very present. Ken and I were attending such a makeup session because I was behind in my physics workbook, which meant we were both behind, and so we both stayed after class and did a little of the required lab work. The teacher stepped out of the room for a while and, feeling restless and bored with studying, I hopped up onto the lab counter and started wrestling and playfully fighting with Ken. I was still standing on the counter and he was standing below me when the teacher came back in the room. I was guilty right then and there, caught red-handed.

Shocked and maybe a little distressed, the teacher stuttered a little and said, "Rrr....rrrobert! You and Kenneth get out and don't come back until after Thanksgiving!"

I was chastised, but fortunately he didn't mean I was kicked out of school, it just meant I couldn't come back for extra classroom work until I controlled myself. It was all just play, of course, but I still liked to blame my behavior on the fact that I was one of the youngest and smallest kids in the class. It may be an excuse, but it did affect me and I never took organized sports seriously because I figured I had a disadvantage with my height. So I continued to have a bit of a rambunctious personality throughout school to compensate, but I was grateful to have Ken as a friend because he didn't seem to mind.

Ken was a great person for saving face. He had his ideas on some things that I didn't share, but it didn't bother me. One thing was, however, that you never wanted to act like you were weak, or cry or tear up in his world. But, there again, being smaller and younger I had the tendency to show more emotion sometimes. On my report card one year in grade school a teacher had written a negative remark about something regarding my behavior. When I asked her about it she said that I had been whispering in class and I started to tear up a little at her criticism. Her heart momentarily softened, she hurriedly added that we could probably erase that remark, so being more emotional wasn't always a bad thing. Nevertheless, Ken said that if I was ever teary around him we would tell people it was because he hit me.

Another moment of my immaturity nearly cost me dearly. It was a nice, sunny weekend and Ken and I were returning from shooting gophers. I had my little H&R 22-revolver still loaded, thinking I might see a gopher or two before getting back into town. I didn't see any though, and so we drove back to my house and relaxed and chatted near the garage for a while. Ken had a passion for whipping out his revolver and pointing it at me just like he was a quick draw gun-slinger from frontier days. That made him happy, but it was a dangerous thing to do. My usual response was to point my gun at his guts and pull the trigger, which was even more dangerous.

Ken was standing up beside the garage and I was lying on the ground. He pulled his gun out and did his usual quick draw. I, of course, had to respond to his invitation and instead of taking the gun out of the holster since I was lying on my shoulder, I merely reached down and pulled the trigger while tipping the holster up at an angle toward Ken. To my shock the forgotten bullet from the ride home exited through the end of the holster and passed in between Ken's outstretched legs and into the garage. Mortified and shocked that I'd done such a dumb thing, I was at the same time relieved that I hadn't hit Ken. It had been so close, but it hadn't happened. After we settled down a little bit, we considered it a miss as good as a mile, but that was certainly a cardinal mistake and I never did a trick like that again. It would have ruined my life and would have been a life threatening moment for Ken and could have been his last quick draw. Of course, my folks and his folks had no inkling of what had happened, and we sure didn't tell them.

Ken and I both managed to stay alive and keep our grades up to graduate high school, and we started attending Montana State University (now The University of Montana) just a few blocks down the road in the fall of 1940. Ken still tended to be more outgoing than me and, therefore, I had fewer friends and would strike up a friendship less than he would. I was also pretty shy with girls, they seemed to be more mature and saw me more as a kid than someone their age. Ken liked the girls, but he continued to go along with me quite a bit.

Ken in all his glory with his 22 and 45 revolvers
Drinking Pepsi and eating butterhorns

Although university life was busy, we managed to go out on a few adventures and one summer we wanted to explore water sports so we bought ourselves a kayak. As a kid before I met Ken, I'd forced myself to take private swimming lessons out at the university to get a little more comfortable with the water. My brother Bill was a good swimmer and one of his favorite things was to get together with his buddies and go swimming in the Bitterroot River. He also thought it was cool to go skinny dipping when conditions were such that they could go unadorned without freezing, though I never did follow in his footsteps when it came to that. In fact, I wasn't a great swimmer at all, but I could at least dog paddle. At the university Ken had to take two years of swimming courses, we all did as a requirement, but neither of us were very good swimmers. Occasionally he and I would go out toward Mill Town near the power dam that blocked the Clark Fork River, slip into the water, and paddle along close to the banks in normal water conditions, though we would never venture too far.

Our kayak was canvas and had a light framework, and we thought it was really something. It was a mail order kit from Montgomery Ward. Lightweight pieces of wood created the frame and canvas was stretched over the frame snuggly. Then we used a can of sealant to saturate it, making it waterproof, and as it dried it shrunk to a tight fit. There was a very small plywood seat and a small piece of plywood flooring. The whole kayak was about eight feet long, and included in the kit were two paddles.

By this time an old friend of mine hung out with us from time to time. This was Glen Halm, the younger brother of Bill's friend Ed. Ken didn't care much for him though. He wasn't too good in school, though later he became quite a proficient lumber grader. Glen would show up at Ken's now and then and Ken put up with him because he was an old friend of mine, but gradually we weaned away from him. On this summer day, though, all three of us decided to go kayaking on the Bitterroot River. The river was still pretty swift after the spring thaw, and three of us were just too many for the lightweight kayak. Glen was in the middle, Ken was in the back with a paddle and I was in the front paddling. Being right up front I could see we weren't controlling it too well. The current wanted to take us under a large branch, something I knew would spell disaster.

Paddling like mad to get out of the current, we got a little ahead of the branch, but Glen started panicking, saying, "We're gonna sink! We're gonna sink!"

Ken's mouth was clenched shut and I didn't say anything either and both of us continued to row for our lives. Finally nearing the edge of a low bank I leapt out and stabilized the front end of the kayak. Grabbing Glen's hand, I gave him a big pull up. Ken was last and as I pulled him up I saw that he was quite pale, but he didn't say a word. Later he told me he was thankful for me pulling him out and I knew then just how scared he had been. With his personality he wasn't going to act like it, but he was pretty scared and I'd never seen him quite like that before.

Leaving the river and heading back to the road, I talked Ken into making a trip to a lookout in the area of Arlee on the Flathead Indian Reservation, just north of town. We were trying to copy what my brother Bill had done with his car and friends. He often hosted his friends with his Model A Ford up to lookouts and endured the rough rocky roads up at higher elevations. Bill was kind of a dreamer and he dreamed about being an explorer. This rubbed off on me a little bit, as I often wanted to do what Bill was doing, and so Ken and I found ourselves driving up to the lookout in Ken's Model A. His Model A was in poor condition, but we didn't really realize it at the time. Our destination wasn't too high in the hills, but when we were coming back toward Missoula the engine suddenly started knocking badly. We quickly pulled over, shut down the engine, and checked the oil. The dip stick showed no oil at all, but there was evidently a slight amount still left in the engine. Nevertheless, we knew we couldn't continue very far under that condition. Fortunately, or just dumb luck, we were right at the edge of the town of Arlee and found a service station there. We managed to drive around the back of the station and yes, there was a big open barrel of used oil that they had collected from oil changings and yes, there was a jar that we could use to scoop up some of the oil. We poured that used black oil into Ken's engine, and Lord knows what all went in there. It was open to the air and rain water and all sorts of things, but that was the oil we used and somehow we made it back to

Missoula. We learned our lesson again in that instance and never tried to push the limits of Ken's poor old Model A again.

Bill and I were getting older, but before we were old enough to fly the coop and leave home our family of four took a two-week trip in our Model A Sedan to California in 1939. Our Aunts Pat and Dolorous, Mom's sisters, lived there, but our ultimate goal was to visit members from both Mom and Dad's sides of the family and to see the 1939 World's Fair at Treasure Island in the San Francisco Bay. The island was manmade and dredged out to form an island adjacent to the existing landscape. It was quite an attraction.

To get all the way to San Francisco we had to drive across much of the western United States and got to take in its natural beauty and wildness. From Missoula we drove through Yellowstone Park with its unique geysers and busy wildlife, and then we went on through the Grand Teton Park and were delighted to see the picturesque, sharp, snow-covered Teton peaks along the way. Wildlife was abundant there as well, and driving at night we had to be careful not to collide with elk, though they weren't the only wildlife we came across on the road. On our way toward Salt Lake City we encountered a mass of so-called Mormon crickets that covered the entire road for nearly a mile or two. That was definitely a new experience for all of us. Smashed beneath the wheels, the crushed crickets made for very slick conditions and we had to drive slowly and carefully. We managed to continue though the crickets and got to see some of the unusual beauty of the colorful sandstone spires and eroded rock towers of Bryce Canyon and Zion National Parks. This area was also native to the Navajo, and it was interesting to see their thatched stands and artifacts.

Nevada had its own natural beauty of desert cactus and vegetation, but what impressed me were the large desert jackrabbits. Just before dusk in the late afternoon dozens of them grouped up in circles of six or seven like they were having clan meetings. The sheer quantity of the jackrabbits really impressed me, they were everywhere we looked.

Entering California was quite the change in landscape, and many of the nicer homes we passed each had their own swimming pool. Being country boys and not used to that type of living, my brother and I thought that was pretty extravagant. Upon arrival all of the relatives treated us royally, and when we went to the World's Fair there was so much to see we were pretty tired by the time we left in the evenings. It was quite an extensive trip for our family and it really opened my eyes to the diversity of our small part of the world.

In the spring of 1941 my brother Bill left for active duty with the army air corps. Many of his friends were either already in or were soon to be in the armed forces, and during this time World War II was picking up speed in Europe and in the Pacific, though the U.S. was still on the sidelines. I wished I had given Bill more companionship in those few years before he left for the army because I was gradually realizing more and more what a neat brother he was. We eagerly devoured his letters from his first experiences as an aviation cadet. Bill's letters were so detailed and we could see that he would shine early on in the flying part of the training. His instructors enjoyed having him as a student because he took to it so avidly and with great results. His letters were modest, but you could see he was going to be a great pilot.

When Bill was in advanced flying school at Luke Field near Phoenix in Arizona he was due to graduate December 12th, 1941 and he wanted the folks to come down to see him graduate because he thought that might be the last time before he'd go overseas. He wanted me to go too, but my grades were very poor at the university and it was at a time just before finals so I said I couldn't make it. I know that disappointed him, and Mom couldn't drive so that meant Dad had to drive the V8 down all by himself. His health was beginning to fail a bit and the drive must have been quite tiring and was not the best idea. Of course, when Japan struck Hawaii at Pearl Harbor on December 7th that threw everything for a loop, and the United States soon declared war first on Japan and then on Germany and Italy. Bill had previously been scheduled to continue working as an instructor pilot alongside his own former instructor, something he was really looking forward to. He was a natural for instructing and he had a pride and desire to try to do his best for his students. When Pearl Harbor struck he still graduated, but his orders for being an instructor were out the window. It changed the picture. He had a hurried visit with Mom and Dad at graduation and immediately afterwards he and most of his group reported for duty in California. There was a fear that the Japanese might attempt an attack along the coast and they needed to get the airplanes up and patrolling in that area. Bill continued writing letters as often as he could, but things were different now, more serious, and he adapted that attitude wholeheartedly. Soon after-wards he was deployed to England to fight in the war, and later to North Africa.

Bill after flying is P-38 to England in 1942

During my first year of university in the fall of 1940 I still didn't know what I wanted to do with my life. Most of my friends had their lives planned out. Some people immediately wanted to sign up and enlist in the military and my old friend Warren Heyer was one of them, gung ho to join the Navy. I was still taking science classes like Ken, though I didn't really enjoy it. I mostly just did what was required of me at the university, such as ROTC basic training. By the time the attack on Pearl Harbor occurred and the U.S. declared war, I knew it was only a matter of time until I would also get caught in the draft.

Here I was in Missoula, far away from any war, but my brother was already gone, and so, not sure what else to do, I followed in his footsteps and signed up with the United States Army Air Corps on May 25th, 1942 in the spring of my sophomore year. This required going through civilian pilot training at the university. The program was to get university sophomores in their spring quarters and give them approximately 40 hours of flying experience and a basic course in weather, theory of flight, civil air regulations, and other topics pertinent to successful flying and to fulfil the requirements for a private flying license before being sent off to the army for further training.

The first step in this was to take a physical fitness test and a fairly extensive written examination where they tested us on general knowledge and intelligence on a varied scale. A friend of mine at the university, Jay Lockhart, decided to take the same route as me as well as a dozen or more applicants in Missoula. It was a fairly extensive test that lasted a couple of hours. After the results were available, we checked our scores. In anticipation I eagerly looked over the results and discovered that my score was actually quite high and it was identical to Jay's. That pleased me quite a bit because Jay's whole family was made up of brains. He had an older brother who was very sharp and a younger sister, and all of them appeared to be very intelligent. I certainly wasn't a scholar, but I was pleased at any rate with the results.

Civilian pilot training was with a little Piper Cub. I had a hard time with that airplane and I didn't take to flying like Bill did. We flew out from a field adjacent to the fairgrounds called Hale Field, and, as it was no runway, there were quite a few dips and bumps in it. When I tried taking off it was like riding a bucking bronco and it overwhelmed me a bit. I thought I was a fairly good outdoorsy guy, but this was entirely new. Slow to take charge, it took me ten hours before I could go up by myself and some people were doing it at eight hours. Not only was taking off a challenge, but landing was as well. As I got closer to the field I thought, boy, when I come in on that one runway I'm going to have to clear the fairgrounds and the hanger…that's going to be scary.

I was a bit of a worry brow and so my grades from my instructor were not ideal.

His name was Bill Yaggy. He was a tall laid-back guy, very easy-going. The authorities at the school probably realized I needed more of an experienced instructor and one that was more demanding, so I was soon assigned someone new and he wasn't particularly the friendly type. This was better for me in the end because he sure got me whipped into enough shape so I could solo and continue learning. On one occasion, when I was pretty well along in the training, an older pilot known well in Montana aviation was giving me a check ride to test me on a few things. We went up and I was told to perform a spin, which I did.

"What are you doing!" he yelled. "You hardly looked around before pulling something like that!" He immediately gave me hell for not making a tough enough inspection for other airplanes in the air, which was, of course, a very valid and important procedure. I didn't make that mistake again after that. He didn't criticize my flying as much as he did that incident, and so in the end I graduated with the others although I had needed more hours than some. But graduating did give me quite a needed leg-up to boost my confidence when I got into Army Aviation a few months later.

After Bill left for the army air corps I inherited his Model A Ford. Overall the car didn't have a great deal of bulk, it was pretty simple. Three people could sit in the front seat, though it was fairly crowded, and it had a seat in the back. You just turned up the handle on the back portion and it folded back, making a back rest called the rumble seat. It was large enough for two people. Bill's Model A was a pretty cool little machine, a roadster. Its name: The Dynamiter, or Dyna as we called it sometimes. It had dynamite power. Bill had worked with the help of dad and some of his friends to put in an 85 horsepower V8 engine, which gave it twice the power of a regular Model A. But unfortunately he changed the rear-axil gears to a higher range, which decreased its ability to climb steep mountains. This proved to be a handicap later on. Dyna also had a neat little folding canvas top. The framework was adequate and you could put it together pretty quickly. It was a durable, sturdy fabric, and water repellant. We didn't have any side protection from wind or rain, but it was a very efficient little outfit.

It was around November that Glen Halm and I copied something Bill had done. We drove past Lolo Hot Springs, it was winter and there was snow on the ground. We drove as far as we could with Dyna. We didn't have chains and when the road became too steep we had to stop and turn around so we'd be facing downhill when we returned. We borrowed our brothers' skis and slowly skied uphill a few miles to a forest service cabin at Lolo pass, which was on the border of Montana and Idaho. We had the keys and permission to use the cabin overnight and had brought along a little food. There was also some bedrolls there that we could utilize so we didn't have to pack any bedding. We played around in the snow and did a little skiing, taking pictures. Good old Shep was there too and seemed to be enjoying playing in the snow as much as we did.

We started back the next day probably a little later than we should have. Although the road was all downhill, which made it easier to ski, it had snowed a little more and there were two or three inches of fresh snow on the top of Dyna by the time we got back down to the car on our skis. It was getting toward dusk and we hopped in, but when we turned the key the car just groaned. The temperature was probably well below freezing, possibly fifteen or twenty degrees Fahrenheit. Well that was bad news, it was too dark and cold to ski back up to the cabin and we didn't have any blankets in the car because we had slept up there. So Glen, Shep and I snuggled together briefly in the seat but I could see that wasn't going to work. It really was too cold to try to spend the night there.

Then I suddenly had the idea to build a little fire under the car and heat up the engine. It was dangerous though, if we got too big a fire it would ignite the engine and also any dripping gasoline could add to the flames. Everything was snow covered but we knew enough to scrounge around the closer trees and get little dried branches from underneath or wherever we could. I crawled under the car and cleared away the previous snowfall, which wasn't too hard to do, and fortunately I had fire equipment and matches. It wasn't long until we had a pretty good little fire, but I knew I had to keep it small. Keeping watch on it from time to time, we got back in the car and waited to see what the result would be.

After about twenty minutes we decided to give it a try. We turned on the ignition and, yes, we had a functioning machine. The engine turned over nicely. It had no doubt heated up the battery, as well as the oil pan and oil, to get started up. So we drove back down and on to Missoula. It was dark, but we had no further problems.

The next day when my dad learned of this he said, "Bob, I'm not going to worry about you anymore."

I grinned broadly. He thought that was pretty good survival and I was rather pleased myself with how well it turned out.

Only nineteen years old and now experienced with my new car and more confident in myself, I wanted to explore more. Even though our country was at war, it hadn't quite registered with me yet, and I wanted to do something adventurous before being called up for duty. Ken wasn't the only one with a Model A anymore, I now had the Dynamiter, and all I needed was a destination and a few travel companions. Ken's mom, being the business woman she was, had now moved the family to a big two story home on Daly Avenue near the university and rented out some of the rooms to university students to bring in more income. Other houses in the area did the same thing, and this was where Ken met Clark MacDonald and introduced him to me. With the summer of 1942 around the corner, the three of us began plotting our longest and grandest road adventure ever: Mexico.

Part 2:

Mexico

Me, Clark MacDonald, Ken Rigby – August 1942
Sporting our pith helmets

The older I got, the more I realized how much I was influenced by my brother Bill. I had my friends, he had his, and we both had our own lives, but when he and two other friends decided to go on a five-week road trip to Mexico, I figured I had to do the same with mine. Bill and his friends planned to go to Mexico in Bill's Model A Ford, the Dynamiter, when they were in their early years at the university. He and his friends, Fred Barrett and Micky Thieme, all took Spanish in high school and so they could speak it fairly well, whereas when I took my friends we knew zip about the language. We brought a Spanish-English dictionary along and we already knew the word *gracias*, we had that word down pat, so we thought we were set. Bill took his trip in the summer of 1940 and I followed in his footsteps with my friends Ken and Clark two years later.

Ken, or 'the duke' as I now called him from time to time, since he often dressed up, was balding a bit at the top at the time of our trip. He was still taller than the rest of us, but in the intervening couple years he had gotten to follow my lead on things. Because of some of my close calls as a child and teenager, I was now the one who was cautious and looked out for things. To say the least, he wasn't so much inclined that way. Clark, originally from Great Falls, attended Montana State University with the rest of us in Missoula. He was renting a room near Ken and was a sophomore in 1942, same as us. Ken broached the topic of going to Mexico and Clark was really enthused about it. He wanted to enjoy a foreign scene and was also gearing up to go on a grand adventure himself.

I didn't know Clark very well though. Once we started talking about the trip we got together in our spare time at the university and I went over to Ken's a lot of the time. Since Clark lived around there as well we slowly got acquainted. Still a bit unsure about him, I often thought to myself that since Ken and Clark knew each other they could get together and overrule me on what we did, but I had nothing to fear. It turned out that I was yet again the unofficial leader. I had the car, which I had inherited from Bill. I don't recall ever paying him for it, but the car was mine now. I also had the knowledge of what Bill did, and I took over. I was the youngest, but not by much, and it turned out there was no animosity on the whole trip. We had invited another couple friends to go but that would have been a disaster. There would have been no room to start with because of all the gear piled in the back on the rumble seat, so it worked out that they couldn't go and it was great with just the three of us.

After weeks of plotting and planning we had the Dynamiter all packed up and were ready to go. Here we were, our country at war with the Axis of Japan, Germany, and Italy, and I had the audacity to plan to go ahead with this trip we had scheduled. I was finished with Civilian Pilot Training and had already signed up with the army air corps to train as a flying cadet. The army had said they wouldn't be able to call us up until Thanksgiving or Christmas because of the big backload of building bases and training facilities, so I figured that left plenty of time for me to do the trip since it was summer. Clark had also already signed up with the coast guard to attend a machinist course in diesel mechanics and allied subjects in New York City, but that wasn't to begin until December. Ken, although he was strong and tall, had had serious health problems earlier in his life and was rated 4F by the military, meaning he was listed in a category where he wouldn't be called up to active duty because of multiple health problems. Basically it wasn't good. Mostly he had suffered chronic bronchitis and had already endured two double mastoid operations.

So, in theory, all three of us were cleared to go. I knew I was sworn in but I didn't realize I was actually enlisted as a private in the army reserve awaiting activation. The army didn't state any restrictions. We were just supposed to be available on notice. That turned out to shorten our trip in the end, but let's start at the beginning.

We left Missoula for Great Falls on August 5th, 1942. Ken and I drove over to where Clark lived on a wheat ranch with his mom, dad, and younger brother and stayed overnight. It was right during the harvest. I didn't realize at the time what trauma it probably gave his parents when he left on this trip. Already there was a shortage of manpower on the ranch, especially for someone who could drive expensive machinery. Clark left a real void there. However, his family said nothing to us and had no problems with us staying overnight, and the next morning we left for Yellowstone Park through the north entrance in the direction of Mammoth Hot Springs. Our journey had begun.

We camped most every day, though we didn't have sleeping bags. We had one bedroll with full blankets and pillows and a tarp that we could stretch over the car in case of rain, but that was it. We just slept out in the open that way. That first night in Yellowstone we settled under our blankets, excited and exhausted about the start of our new adventure, but things were just getting started. We camped in an unauthorized spot because we didn't want to pay a fee for a campsite and soon learned why there were

designated camping areas. I awoke in the middle of the night to a deep rumbling, and then a growl. Before even looking around I knew what it was, a bear. And guess whose side he came up on? Yours truly. Now, my mother had baked a small cherry pie for us in a small frying pan. For some reason, we had that laying around out under the tarp and this darn black bear had found the pie and whisked it away. We never did find any remnants of it the next day, but he had it cleaned slick as a whistle, I'm sure.

Fortunately the bear was younger, but he had claws on him and teeth and he wanted more. He came back over to my side and I waved my arms around.

The Intruder

47

"Ken! Clark!" I yelled, but their only response was to rise up briefly and roll over. They weren't going to wake up. A different plan was needed. I had a small axe with a handle about three feet long and I raised that up over my head as the bear came right to me. It was the middle of the night but there was still enough starlight to see him. He looked at me and I stared back at him. If he came any closer, I was going to hit him on the head or wherever I could hit him and try to fend him off. It would have been a little bloody, one way or another. I didn't want to chop on him. If he got injured, we'd have to report it and we'd be fined and it could ruin the whole start of the trip.

The bear and I continued to stare at each other for what seemed like a long time. I don't know what that bear was thinking about, but somehow I was able to stare him down and eventually he turned around and walked on. He was still around the next morning, but didn't come near as close as he had in the night. I didn't give Ken and Clark hell or anything for not waking up, in fact, I didn't tell them much about that night at all. After snapping a few pictures of the little bear, we packed up and went on our way, but they never did know just how bad that first night could have been.

That next day we continued through the park, enjoying the sights and the wildlife. Yellowstone is quite a unique place due to the volcanic activity and geysers, and that paired with all the bison and bears made quite a scene. As we drove I recalled the earlier trip that I'd made with the family to Yellowstone in 1939. In the 1930s they would feed the bears, black bears and grizzlies together, scraps from the food service and hotels in the park. People could watch the event from a few bleachers that stood about a hundred yards or so back. As many as twenty or thirty bears would gather at a time. These bears would squabble briefly, but they were all only really interested in the food. Watching that with my family had been quite a scene. Later, the park realized encouraging bears to rely on humans for food was a disaster, and was also probably a factor in what led to our own little bear encounter, but it was an amazing sight while it lasted.

We kept pretty much on the go. Our second night had another set of problems.

Due to a swarm of mosquitoes we had a rather uncomfortable night, and, slightly sleep deprived the next morning, we headed on through the beautiful Grand Teton National Park in Wyoming. Our discomforts were momentarily distracted when we were greeted in the park by peak after snow-covered peak. They towered over a few elegant lakes. Due to the calmness of the lakes, the mountains were reflected perfectly against them, making their magnificent appearance more grand and vast. It was like looking at a painting.

This was quite the contrast to the rest of our drive through Wyoming. Dry and desert-like, we didn't think it very inviting. It was quite windy and was sagebrush country. In preparation for the trip I had bought three pith helmets for us, utilizing my twenty percent off employee discount at Missoula Mercantile. The helmets were light and comfortable and allowed for good air circulation. They also had a chin strap, which was useful when we were going down the highway with the top down, as we didn't lose them. It might have pointed us out as tourists, but we wore them quite a bit. Despite this I still succeeded in getting a fair sunburn out of our drive through the Wyoming desert. But, with an aching sunburn and itching mosquito bites from Yellowstone, we still managed to get a decent night's sleep near Rock Springs, close to the border with Colorado.

Colorado was a big improvement over the Wyoming desert. Mostly it was nice seeing the color green again. We were heading south toward Denver. Here again, I wanted to copy Bill's steps. He had gone down to Colorado Springs, south of Denver, and had intended to climb Pike's Peak at 14,109 feet, but that was not to be. At that time he had experienced a great deal of trouble with the Dynamiter. He had installed a V8 engine earlier and the radiator, while very classic looking, didn't have near the cooling capacity for such an engine. The result was the car boiled a great deal and he couldn't even attempt to drive all the way up to Pike's Peak. When my turn came around with the Dynamiter I had my dad install the Model B radiator, the predecessor to the V8, and it handled cooling the engine much better. This changed the looks a little on the front end but still it looked quite a bit like the Model A. Bill had also installed a high ring gear in the rear axle of the car. This was way too extreme and meant that the car did not have any downright lugging capacity, and when we were climbing…well it was going to struggle with any intense climbing at all.

All this circled through my mind again as I held the accelerator down to the floorboard for the last mile up to the peak. I hadn't said anything to Clark. He was mechanical and could have maybe adjusted the carburetor to get a more air efficient mixture or something. I had a tendency not to say much when things were going downhill. I figured we'd talk about it when it was a crisis. But Dyna still climbed up the mountain, bit by bit. I was just getting ready to tell the guys they had to get out and push, that she wouldn't go any further, but, dumb luck, we just made it. We were right at the top of the mountain and just as we approached the sign saying "Pike's Peak – 14,109 feet" we were peppered with graupel. It turned the ground white. Despite this, Clark leapt out of the car and snapped a picture of our success at reaching the peak. He unofficially became the main photographer on our trip since he had a lot of previous experience with cameras and equipment and was quite good at finding the shots. Because of the hail we didn't stay very

long on the mountain, and we had already achieved our goal anyway. Pike's Peak was quite the thrill for me, as it was the highest I'd ever been.

Back in Colorado Springs we had to make a stop at a doctor's office. Ken had been having throat problems and had his raw throat swabbed out and treated. He wasn't able to eat for a while afterwards, and on that day Clark and I each had roast beef with mashed potatoes, gravy and all the dressings with a nice coleslaw and ice cream for dessert. It had all just cost us 50 cents each, so Ken missed a really great supper. He didn't complain but we should have saved some for him for when he was feeling better. One event did distract him from his pain for a little while, however. The entire next day was spent traveling east across 400 miles of the dry plains of Kansas. As we approached the eastern border with Missouri we started to get into the Bible belt a little and came across a sign that said "The wages of sin is death." Ken, being a gun nut, had taken along his 32-nickel-plated revolver. It had a broken firing pin and there were no bullets, but he thought it would be useful if you had to scare or bluff somebody. Of course, we could have gotten into a lot of

trouble pulling that out against somebody who actually had a fully functioning revolver, but again I figured we'd talk about it if it became a crisis. We didn't say anything to him and he kept it hidden, somewhere in the back seat. At any rate, Ken and Clark thought that sign would be a good opportunity for a picture and Ken got down on his knees in front of the sign like he was praying for mercy and Clark held the gun to his head. I snapped the picture and laughed, shaking my head.

From there we headed on into Missouri. When we came to Concordia we found a city park. It was shaded, had rest spots and camping spots, welcomed campers, and it was free. We thought that was pretty neat. It had better facilities than usual as we didn't often have water available. On this particular day there was a paddlewheel steamboat along the bank and three friendly girls came along through the camp.

They were of a suitable age for us guys and after a bit of small talk one asked, "Would you all like to come to the dance with us this evening?"

"It's on the steamboat," another of the girls added shyly, pointing out towards the river.

I immediately shrunk back a little. In this situation I pictured myself sitting on the sidelines while the other guys danced. I hadn't dated much and was shy with the girls. Clark was quite the ladies' man though.

"Well I don't know about me," I began, "but you two go on ahead. It'll be fun!"

I could see the excitement in Clark's eyes, but then he shook his head. "Ah, well, thanks for the invitation, but perhaps another time," he said.

I told Clark multiple times that he and Ken should go, but they wouldn't do it. And with that, after a few more exchanged words, the girls smiled and walked off. Later, I just shook my head thinking, what a party pooper! I could have watched and been a wallflower for a while, it wouldn't have hurt me. But the boys wouldn't go without me. Clark regretted that later, I could tell, but the opportunity had already passed. Later on I did discover a way to overcome my shyness, but that's another story.

August 13th, 1942
St. Louis, MO

Dear Folks,

Well, we've covered a lot of miles since I wrote to you last and none of us have been writing any letters. Right now I'm in a tourist cabin in St. Louis, which incidentally, is the first cabin we have stayed at.

We got here about 3:30 this afternoon. It's about 9:30 now since we just got through doing our washing at a (public) laundry here in the camp. We put a dime in the washing machine, and it was supposed to run for 25 minutes. However, it ran for an hour on that dime and we were able to get our washing done pretty easily. Tomorrow we will iron out those things that need it.

All of Missouri seems to be green rolling hills and isn't half bad, last night we stayed at Concordia, Mo. It was there where I pulled the gear shift lever out of Dyna. Evidently the cap had come loose and the pin pulled out. But with Clark acting as mechanic we got the thing together again.

About the only other thing that has happened to Dyna is a persistent loose radius rod.

Now for a few questions, etc, for you to answer. – Have you heard from Bill yet? If so what's the news? I haven't written to him yet or anyone else, but I intend to do more writing soon. How's Shep?

Well, I'm getting pretty tired now so I guess I'll quit. But I'll try not to wait so long next time to write.

Love, Bob

From St. Louis we turned south along the Mississippi River and drove into Kentucky. One might be thinking this wasn't exactly the most direct route to Mexico from Montana, but I wanted to say I'd been to Florida, and I was driving. Ken and Clark didn't object, so a few days later, after

Clark at the border

driving over 700 miles cutting through Tennessee and diving deep into Alabama, we arrived on an afternoon in Pensacola, Florida. Lo and behold we were also right by a naval primary flight school. Parking near the fence a little ways from the runway we followed the planes with our eyes as they took off and landed. I watched them soaring through the air and with some apprehension wondered to myself if I could do it or not, fly one of those. They were very impressive. During the war I ended up flying different types of planes anyway, but this was where I first felt that little tinge of concern about what I was getting into in the future. As if linked to my troubled thoughts, the sky suddenly opened up before us. Water was soon gushing along the curbs. It was a flash flood and we sat there a while, waiting for it to pass. The rain was heavy, smashing hard into the ground and immediately drenching everything it touched. We didn't get wet at all though, thanks to the canvas car top. I was protected this time by the thin top of my car and later in the war, in a similar way, by something unseen.

After our little stop in Pensacola we headed in the direction of Laredo, Texas. This was our destination to cross the border into Mexico, though first we had to pass through Mississippi and Louisiana. We went into Mississippi as night was falling. It wasn't raining, but we couldn't find any place off the road to camp. Finally we saw what looked like an open field without a fence. We didn't see any lights around or anything, so we made camp. Laid out in the open next to the Dynamiter we slept like logs. I woke up when the sun was already high in the sky and saw that we were being watched by four or five little black kids. They were gawking at us, not saying a word, marveling at our appearance, our gear, our awkward situation. It was then we noticed a house across the road, though I didn't see any activity over there and they didn't come and see who these intruders were. Feeling slightly embarrassed, we hurriedly packed up and drove on to find a service station to freshen up at.

A few things awaited us in Laredo, Texas. That's where I had told mom and dad to write so we could pick up letters when we arrived and then again when we left Mexico. By this time we also noticed that some of our tires looked a bit out of shape. Ken and Clark had volunteered to buy some used tires for the trip, and now that they were nearly worn down to the fabric we purchased two used General Popos (named after the mountain peak Popocatepetl) on the Mexican side of Laredo. This ended up being one of our good decisions, as Mexico held more adventures for us and the car than we anticipated. Ready to explore the new country, our first goal was, of course, Mexico City.

It was a 700 mile stretch from the border to the capital, which gave us enough time to adapt and experience the new culture before arriving in the big city. At first the landscape was hot and dry, though the roads were in decent shape and gradually climbed to a higher elevation. At one point we decided to stop at one of the many banana stands we saw scattered along the highway. This one was also located near a little dwelling next to some fields. As we got out of the car to stretch and munch on some food we saw several

little kids running around. One of them, a boy, was around two years old. He was the cutest little guy anyone could imagine, with raggedy pants and a cowboy type hat perched on top of his head. I reached around in my pocket until I pulled out a shiny penny. I took that and squatted down and held it on just the tip just so it would reflect in the sunlight. Entranced, he reached out and latched onto it with his little fingers as tight as he could. We had a small game of tug of war for a few moments. I was teasing him a little, but he was determined and he wanted that coin. With a smile on my face I released it and he bounded away joyfully. He didn't know what it was worth, but it was like gold to him. I stood up and watched him run off before going back to the car. He was a cute fellow for sure and full of life. His parents had to be proud of him, he was a dandy!

There was vacant land all along the highway, and so it wasn't hard finding a place to pull over off the road a ways and get a good night's sleep in our customary manner. We never had any problems with snakes or lizards or other critters interfering with our sleep, though one morning Ken was looking rough and struggled a bit getting into his clothes. I couldn't help but laugh at him and snap a picture in his disarray. He was a good sport about it all, nonetheless, and soon we were on our way again.

After a few days of travel we got to the outskirts of Mexico City and were stopped at an entry station. The men taking our information were in uniforms and we took them to be police. They checked us out a little, examining our car and our faces, and said we should follow them. We were slightly nervous and wondered about just how official this all was, but we followed anyway. It was a good idea as they showed us a place to stay for the evening, which would end up being our haven for the next three nights. We were now on the edge of Mexico City.

August 25th, 1942
Mexico City

Dear Mother and Dad,

Well how are you? I'm fine. We are staying at a nice hotel apartment here in Mexico City. We arrived here yesterday afternoon after about three days travel from the border.

There are certainly some interesting sights to see along the road. Most of it is different from anything I've ever seen. The people, houses, and scenery are all different from anything we saw in the U.S.

The road heads up some really fine looking country after leaving Monterrey for some distance. The mountains are quite high and the road is fairly steep in some places, but it is kept in good repair.

We're beginning to get used to being in a foreign country somewhat, and it doesn't bother us so much to have Spanish spoken by most of the people around us. Along the Pan-American Highway we usually ate at a restaurant where we could, (recommended Spanish-American places). The food is usually very good and the prices are quite reasonable. So far we are making our own breakfast such as it is. We bought some canned goods at Laredo, Texas and that helps.

The Polly Apartments

When we arrived here yesterday we decided to take this apartment after some indecision because of its cost of 12 pesos or $2.40. It is certainly worth it, but we have to try to keep somewhat within our limits. We'll probably stay here at least another day, however, because it is so nice and so convenient.

We washed our clothes out last night by hand and it was quite a job – we're glad we don't have to do that often.

We spent the most of yesterday afternoon looking around the city – mainly window shopping. However I think it might buy a Navajo-like rug if I can find a pretty good one at a reasonable price. It would be kind of nice in one of the bedrooms, maybe by the writing desk. Don't you think so? I won't be able to hear from you in time so don't let it worry you.

Well we've got quite a bit to do and not a lot of time to do it so I'll sign off for now.

Love, Bob

We stayed about three days in the Polly Apartments. It was a narrow building about five stories tall. The owners were accustomed to tourists and were friendly. In fact, everyone was very gracious. It was quite nice, well-appointed and had very good beds. Since we were used to camping, it was quite the luxury for us. But we were such cheapskates we decided to do our laundry by hand, which was something I hoped never to do again! With some cord we were able to string our clothes up about the room there. Three tired travelers, we enjoyed a nice sleep that night, though we were probably mostly exhausted from scrubbing and wringing out our clothes.

The next morning we got our money, traveler's checks, exchanged into pesos and set off to explore the city. Bill had advised me earlier that it was customary for people to pay ten cents to the small boy who would appear when you parked your car. He would keep a watchful eye on it so that no harm came to it and that nobody tried to steal anything from the car while it was parked under his care. My brother's experiences and advice helped a lot on our trip, helping us with everything from where we should go to what we should buy. Earlier we had also signed up with the Pemex Travel Company and had brought along some of their brochures and pamphlets about Mexico, which were also helpful.

We didn't end up doing too much driving in Mexico City, the traffic could be a little fast and furious, and so we spent a few days simply walking around the business sector of Mexico City. I didn't end up buying a rug like I had mentioned to my parents, but got a few other souvenirs like a machete, typically used for cutting sugar cane, and a few smaller trinkets.

One thing we definitely wanted to do was go to a bull fight. The day we went it was a hot afternoon with good crowds. The fight was brutal, and every now and then the crowds would swell up into a roar of *olé!,* which was exhilarating.

Our next objective was Acapulco on the west coast. My brother, when he took his Mexico trip, had stated he wanted to go to the Gulf Coast and experience the hot steamy jungles. That had absolutely no appeal to me, so I arbitrarily set Acapulco on the Pacific as our goal and nobody objected, as usual. We talked some about where we would go, but everyone seemed to accept that I had an idea of where to go and how to get there, so they mostly followed my lead.

And so, as we continued west, we began a pretty good descent down toward the coastal region. The road we were on was a well-paved, two-lane highway in good condition, with some winding as it declined. We arrived on the beach near Acapulco in the afternoon, the sun high over the ocean. It looked pretty gorgeous. The road first came to a

large sandy beach and we spotted a hotel in the distance. The ocean was a beautiful piercing blue against the horizon and it called to us, we had to stop. The beach was very inviting, no one else was there and it gently sloped into the sea. We parked the car, took off our shirts and pants, and jumped in. We had reached our destination. Clark was the only one who had brought a bathing suit, Ken and I hadn't even thought about it, but we seemed content jumping around in the waves in our underwear shorts. It was a very pleasant temperature, the sun was bright and the water was warm. We definitely needed the refreshment.

In the Pacific

Ken tries the trickle-down theory

We were all feeling a little weak and had been getting low on food since our main standby was bread and peanut butter, and occasionally canned foods. Other than that we relied on a decent restaurant, though we were starting to run low on cash as well.

After we had lounged on the beach a while, we eventually had to listen to our stomachs and go over to the hotel to see if we could get anything to eat. There was hardly anyone there, but we went in, walked to their restaurant area and they were open.

"Can we get some food?" I asked in English hopefully.

"*Si*, yes, *si*, come in!" Our host answered and led us to a table. After a while he came back with an odd smelling dish. I tasted it briefly and noticed that the butter was rancid. The three of us pushed our forks around the plate a little and looked at each other. I waited for the waiter to come by again.

"Don't you have any American food?" I asked.

"Oh, yes!" The man said hurriedly and graciously brought us something more recognizable to our American taste. It especially tasted good after all our canned meals and peanut butter sandwiches.

Once we had enjoyed our time on the beach we turned around and drove back up north toward Mexico City. I can't understand why we didn't drive on in to see the little village of Acapulco. We were low on food and could have used some other supplies, but we didn't go. The only excuse I have is that we were just like Lewis and Clark when they reached the Pacific Ocean, feeling simple relief and exhaustion at having reached the ocean after such a struggle. We, of course, didn't have quite the problems or struggles they had suffered, but we definitely felt a similar sensation of finality after reaching the Pacific ourselves.

Not stopping to resupply was one of our bad decisions, but that's what we did. We found out just how bad an idea it was not much later. It was night now, and we were going up a mountain grade in the dark. We were heading out to the plateau area and there was not much else around. Abruptly the car started sputtering and quit on us right in the middle of the dark highway. Pulling over as best we could on the side of the road, we just sat in silence for a while. We were out of gas: a disaster. Although I'd said to myself I'd speak up when it came to a crisis, and it certainly was a crisis now, we already knew what the trouble was and nothing more needed to be said. Surprisingly, none of us said a word at all. Each of us was deep in our own thoughts and not a word was said. Only a few minutes later we heard a rumbling behind us. Two big trucks with stake beds on them drove up in the night, with probably about twenty people in each truck in the back. They stopped. The drivers hopped out and came over to see what the trouble was.

I jumped out and Ken came with me, holding a flashlight as I dug out the Spanish-English dictionary. How I thought I'd find anything with that I don't know.

"Can you um.....er...." I started, fumbling through its pages. "Um.....our *coche*...." I wasn't getting anywhere and it was obvious that neither of the drivers spoke English. Despite my noble efforts, the dictionary wasn't much help. Then I pointed to our gas cap, which was on the hood just below the windshield.

"Ah!" They nodded, they understood. So they got a hose out from the closest truck, put one end in their gas tank, took our cap off and put a hose in our gas tank and proceeded to fill it. Not just with a little fuel, no, they filled it completely full and didn't spill a drop. Then they put the hose away. I got out my bill fold to try and pay them.

"No, no, no," the driver said, waving his hand kindly. They wouldn't take any money but you can bet we were all speaking *gracias, gracias, gracias*, profusely. They laughed and waved and drove on ahead of us. So my guardian angel was looking out for me again with perfect timing. It was wonderful, a life saver. That could have been quite a hassle.

We continued on up the road. We wanted to get to higher country, where it leveled off more. It was still dark when we got up a ways, a nice night to say the least, but very dark. We pulled over off the road. It was fairly level ground, but open as far as one could see in the starlight.

"Let's camp here," I said, satisfied. The others nodded and bounded out of the car to get things set up. Off in the distance we saw a big bonfire. People were singing and dancing and having a grand old time.

"Do you want to check it out?" Clark asked, noticing the look on my face. Those people were having such a good time…I thought maybe it would be neat to take part in that. The people on the road we met had been so nice, after all. But my cautious side took the better of me.

"Well, it would only take one bad apple in the whole bunch to take advantage of us, only one guy with a knife…" I started hesitantly.

"If something happened we could always explain ourselves with that dictionary," Ken offered with a smirk.

"Shut up, Ken," I said light-heartedly and tossed a pillow at him. "Let's just get to bed." So we got the bedding out and slept like logs again, never hearing anything further that night.

Our rumbling stomachs woke us up the next morning. We needed to resupply our food, and fast. That was the number one priority. Again I kicked myself for not stopping and getting supplies in Acapulco when we had the chance, but we couldn't go back now. However, we were satisfied, and our next destination was to be Mt. Popocatepetl. There again, we were following Bill's agenda.

As we continued away from Acapulco we began to see more dwellings and small roadside stands and better looking restaurants, so we were able to satisfy our hunger and stock up on our bread and canned food again. It wasn't too hard to locate the road that led to Mt. Popo. It was a winding dirt road and fairly steep in places, but we had no trouble traveling upward. We arrived in the early evening and we found a decent spot to camp. It was quite cool and we thought it would be nice to have a small campfire. There were a few tree limbs here and there, mostly smaller ones that were scattered. The problem was we couldn't get anything to burn. I got out the can of white gas we carried for our camp stove. Pouring a little bit on a branch I tried to light it, but it wouldn't start. Frost covered the edges and moisture had penetrated deeper, and thus there was no way we were going to have a fire. So it was a cold night, but it was clear and I could pick out the Milky Way in the stars.

The next morning was foggy and Ken wasn't feeling too good with his sore throat. It had started acting up again. He had to watch that and, as he didn't want to be out trampling around getting worse, he stayed with the car while Clark and I walked the road a little ways. We could see it was blocked with slides of gravel and rocks. Hiking up the side of the mountain we got into the snow pretty quickly. It was cold and the fog was thicker.

"Sure is chilly out here," Clark said, staring up toward the mountain peak. We shivered and took a few more hesitant steps. All I had on was my little light blue polyester jacket. It was one that Bill was issued at primary flight school at Oxnard, California, and on a visit home he had left the jacket with me since he was moving on to his next round of training. I really liked the jacket, but it wasn't particularly built to be worn to hike up the

snowy side of a mountain.

"I suppose we have achieved our mission," I started to say. "We are at Mt. Popo."

Clark nodded in agreement. "No need to make a mountain adventure out of it."

Satisfied with our decision, we snapped a few photos for proof of our achievement. Clark was able to set the timer on the camera with the tripod so we could both be in it, and we tromped back through the snow and fog to the car and Ken.

"Want to head back down?" Ken asked when we were in earshot.

"Yeah," I said, "Let's have a look at the map."

Carefully folding out our map of Mexico, we studied it to find the best way down from Mt. Popo. Our next goal was to get to the city of Puebla. The map showed a few roads heading down from the mountain, but nothing pointed exactly in the direction of where we wanted to go.

"Now wait a minute," I said, looking closer at the map. "This dotted line here heads more in the direction of Puebla, what if we took that?"

The others looked at the map, then back at me, and didn't object. It looked like a definite shortcut, and I could tell the boys, especially Ken, were ready to be off the mountain. We soon learned that dotted lines are dotted for a reason. The car wasn't going to go down that trail with much success. It was like an ox trail, uneven and steep, and just not really meant for our Dyna. It was risky. We didn't get too far down when we came to a big sinkhole, which took up a good part of the trail.

"Think we can get around it?" Clark asked, next to me.

I furrowed my brows determinedly and put it in gear. I got off on the high side as far as I could, but despite my best efforts the left rear wheel dropped down into the gaping hole.

"Nope," I said matter-of-factly.

So there we were.

We got out our jack and tools, whatever we had, which wasn't adequate. Looking around we found a big branch not far from us that had been stripped of leaves and twigs. It looked like it had been used before, and left here for just such an occasion, for those who had encountered what we had. The car wasn't too heavy, so we thought by using the fulcrum principle we'd have her out of there in no time. Then it started raining. I laughed and got out the camera.

"Why are you doing that?" Clark objected.

"We're gonna get out of here," I said, turning the camera towards him, "and we'll have this picture to remind us of what we encountered."

Clark shook his head, but after a few big heaves we did indeed, rain and all, get Dyna out and on the trail again.

With all three of us back in the car the rain quit, and gradually the slope wasn't as steep and it got to be a fairly decent way to travel. We knew now it wasn't an actual road but it was evident it had been used as one. Down more toward level country we ran into a little group of twenty or thirty adobe dwellings, all clustered together. However, nobody was around. There was nobody looking out the window, no sign of life, no signs of any kind, no garbage, no dogs barking, no cattle, no nothing. It was just deserted. The windows

in the clay houses also had no glass, and we could have looked right in if we wanted to. We didn't stop and linger, mostly feeling like we'd be trespassing, and the whole place felt a bit eerie. Traveling right through the middle of the dwellings on a narrow road, which just had enough room for one cart or buggy or small car, we sat in silence the whole way, and everyone breathed a quiet sigh of relief once we had left it in our rear view mirror.

As usual I was driving and continued to do so. We knew pretty well the direction of Puebla, and slowly we started encountering more and more people along the road. Most of them were young men decently dressed in white shirts, pants and sandals. I slowed the car up near some of them.

"Puebla?" I asked, pointing in the direction we thought it was. Some nodded, but a few started heading toward us and because I was driving slowly, three of them jumped up on the running board wanting a ride. One leapt up on my side and two were on Ken's side, Clark was in the middle. They pointed in the direction of Puebla and made a hand motion for money, wanting to be paid for guiding us.

"No, no, no," we all said at once, waving our hands defensively. The men didn't move.

"Get off, now," I said firmly, motioning with my hands and starting to speed up a little.

The man on my side jumped off this time and another jumped off on Ken's side, but the last one, also on Ken's side, didn't want to jump off. Reaching into his white shirt, something metal gleamed in the fading light. Without a second thought Ken put his hand in the man's face and pushed him off backwards hard onto the side road, right off the vehicle.

"Get out of here!" Ken and Clark yelled in my direction and I put the pedal to the floorboard.

Not caring much for the details of what had happened, we didn't know what might have ensued and also didn't want to find out, we bolted out of there as fast as we could. Shortly afterwards we finally got onto a main road and headed toward Puebla. I was real glad Ken was on the side he was, I wasn't sure I'd have just pushed a man to the ground, but Ken had seen that something dangerous was going to happen and had acted quickly. We didn't know if the man had carried a gun or a knife, but we hadn't stuck around to find out.

On the outskirts of Puebla we found a supper club. It was getting dark, and we were hungry. As I parked the car and we got out, Ken noticed that, through the excitement of getting down the mountain, the stitching in the seam of his pants in the back had failed. This created a considerable draft, which was especially noticeable because of the cool night air. The supper club was rather nice, so I went first and Ken followed single file after me, trailed by Clark in order to screen him, though I don't know how much it helped. People probably thought we were a strange bunch, and I felt a lot of eyes on us as we walked in. Most of them were rather well dressed and I can't say the same for us, but nobody gave us any trouble and we were seated without any problems. Our waiter greeted us in a friendly manner and he spoke English to us as well. We had a very tasty meal and, well satisfied, we were ready to be on the road again. Marching out of the restaurant in the same pecking order, ha ha, we hopped back in the car and I started it up. We didn't want to look in the town, we had had enough for one day. We drove fairly fast on the highway in the dark and headed back toward the border, Puebla had been the last stop on our itinerary.

Late morning the next day, before getting to Monterrey on the way to the border, I had another bright idea that turned out to be less bright than planned. We were heading toward a bridge with a river heading underneath it on our left, which caught my attention.

"It looks like we could drive into the water a little ways here and wash the car off," I told the boys. The water was indeed shallow enough and Dyna was no doubt pretty dusty.

"That sounds like a fine idea to me!" Clark said enthusiastically, perhaps a bit dusty himself. So we drove into the water, it was a very shallow grade. It was fairly coarse gravel and therefore I didn't think we'd have any trouble sinking in. We had some sponges with us and started cleaning off the car. I took off my pants and laid them on the bank along with my shoes near where we drove in. Clark did the same thing with his pants and laid them beside my pair on the bank. He put on his bathing suit, and I was just in my

shorts. Ken rolled his pant legs up. After a few minutes I stepped back to admire our work.

"She's looking pretty good, just a little…." I stopped mid-sentence.

There was movement on the riverbank. Two kids, around ten and twelve years old, were each holding a pair of pants in their possession. Our pants. They were taking one last look to see if they were going to get away scot-free, backs half turned toward us.

"Hey!" I yelled, immediately dropping the sponge, and ran after them.

They split up right away and I took off after one of them. I thought I was well enough in shape, but I had to puff pretty hard because he was a pretty good little runner.

"Hey! Stop!" I yelled again.

Finally catching up with him I grabbed him. Wide, terrified eyes looked up at mine and I shook him by the arm, repossessing the pants he had taken. The kid kept yelling to the other one, something I thought was good because then we'd capture both of them and get the other pair of pants back. Thinking all this through, I began to realize that my feet were really hurting. I had sprinted across the hot stones and the dry vegetation and who knows what else to chase this boy with the stolen pants. I started to hobble a little bit. The kid realized I had loosened my grip on his arm and ran from me. A short distance away there was a barbed wire fence and the kid got hung up on that fence momentarily and, boy, did he look like a scared rabbit. I went toward him briefly, but I was hurting so badly that I soon lost all interest in further contact with him. That gave him time to untangle himself and he was soon out of sight. About that time Ken and Clark came running up. I noticed that they had stopped to put on their shoes.

"Did you catch him?" Ken demanded.

I held up the pants, wincing.

"You ok, Bob?" Clark asked.

"Shoes…" I said, motioning towards their feet, "… not a bad idea."

I hobbled towards them, though if I had put on my shoes I probably wouldn't have gotten the pants back at all. As I limped back to the car between them, it turned out that the soles of my feet were completely covered with blood blisters. Ken, unknown to me, had thankfully brought along first-aid supplies. He had had enough contact with doctors and admired how well they bandaged things, so he was able to do quite a job on both my feet.

After bandaging my feet we counted our losses. Ken didn't have any loss because he was still wearing his pants. Clark had had a bill fold and his watch in his pants, and that was the pair I'd rescued. I'd lost my bill fold with my driver's license, my travel card, and a small amount of money. Thankfully I kept my travelers checks in my shirt pocket. Since we recovered at least one pair of pants it wasn't too big a loss except that my ID was gone. I also couldn't drive anymore because of my feet. Propping them out the window showing off Ken's good first-aid work, I let him take the wheel of our newly cleaned car and so passed our final few miles in Mexico.

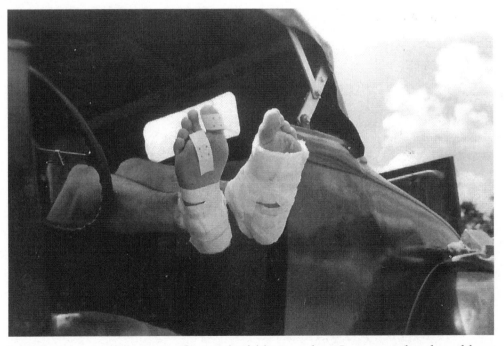

Ken had done a great job on my feet and within two days I recovered and could put on my shoes and drive again. We got to the border in Laredo shortly afterwards, and although I didn't have any ID they accepted my story and let us pass. Before we crossed over we had to switch our tires. We had learned upon entering Mexico that you weren't allowed to bring purchased tires from Mexico into the continental United States because of wartime regulations, and so our General Popos had to go. Before our trip I had bought two new firestone "convoy" tires. They each cost $5.95 on sale, and although my brother probably might forgo such a purchase, I thought otherwise and had snatched them up. They had a deep tread and were just dandy. I hadn't put them on for the trip because Clark and Ken were in charge of the tires. When I found out about the tire situation during our first crossing in Laredo I wired mom and dad and asked them to please send my new firestone "convoy" tires by railroad express. Now that we were entering back through Laredo we could pick up any messages or mail, and those tires were waiting for us when we got there, and they were a godsend. We were so fortunate I had bought those. And also it wasn't too long after we finished the trip that they started rationing gas and other products because of the war, so we were pretty lucky. I thanked my folks, but I should have said *gracias* as well as thank you!

September 6th*, 1942*
Prescott, Ariz.

Dear Mother and Dad,

Well I don't have much time right now to write, but I did need to so here goes.

We received the tires alright in Laredo. They were waiting for us. Thanks a lot!

I haven't received any addresses or telephone numbers yet as you said in your letter. So send me all of the addresses that you think we might possibly need. We're going to Rose's first. We are in Arizona now and we should be in Los Angeles in about 4 days.

Also you can be big about it and send $20 to me in your letter along with the addresses. Send it all by air mail to General Delivery at Los Angeles. I don't think you will have to get a money order. I may be able to make it home on the money I have, but I'm going to have to loan some to Kenneth until he gets home as he can't get in touch with his folks now. Clark is about broke too, but he will be able to get enough for himself in San Francisco.

Please write your letter as soon as you get this. I don't even know Rose's address so if the letter isn't there when we get to L.A. it won't be so good.

We are having a swell time but have spent more money than we intended to. We're coming back by way of California so we won't be able to see Aunt Georgia.

I enjoyed your letter at Laredo. Will write again when better conditions make it easier to do so.

Love, Bob

Back in the United States we were in a bit of a rush. We were running low on cash, it turned out I only ended up spending about $120 on everything, including souvenirs, on the whole trip, but it was still more than we had originally planned. And now we were planning on going up through California. Along the way we did tour some beautiful sites in the Southwest. After driving across Texas we went up to the Carlsbad Caverns in New Mexico and the cliff dwellings of Montezuma Castle in Arizona, which were both marvels to behold. After a quick stop in Prescott to send mail we headed up to the south rim of the Grand Canyon, and from there it was on to California. We had planned to stop in Los Angeles, but having never received the addresses we needed, we headed straight for San Francisco, which would end up being our last stop until home.

Things changed once we got there. We left Clark off at his grandparent's place and Ken and I continued on to my Aunt Pat's. We arrived there later, after supper. It was getting dark. She only had limited bedrooms as she also had two girls, my two cousins. Pat laid out some sheets with blankets and pillows on the carpeted balcony area of their apartment. We had just gotten to sleep about midnight when Pat woke us up.

"Bob," she said, rousing me. "I've got a message from your mother, from the war department."

I sat up quickly. "What did it say?" I asked anxiously.

"It said you're supposed to leave from Missoula within 24 hours for San Antonio, Texas by railroad for active duty." And that was it, I had been nailed, it was my turn to be called up.

Evidently, Mom had received a directive from the war department and had opened it. Worried about what to do she had hesitated calling until the middle of the night. Feeling a sense of duty rise in me, I thought that I could not waste any time. I felt I had to respond immediately, and I did. It really could have waited until morning, but I was the one with the car and Clark had no alternative when I called him and told him I was going to go immediately and that we needed to get on our way home. He was, understandably, shocked, and it was hard for him to explain to his grandparents why he couldn't even stay overnight. I was adamant though and he accepted the situation.

"That's the way it is," he and Ken said as we packed up our things and left. We wasted no time and took the shortest route possible back to Missoula and it wasn't under the best conditions.

We stopped only a few times along the way, mostly to refuel. We wanted to get more supplies in Vallejo, California, but weren't quite sure of the way, and it was dark. Stopping at a small store on the road I walked to the attendant and said,

"Excuse me, we're looking for Valley Joe, are we heading in the right direction?"

"Where?" the attendant asked, confused.

"Valley Joe?" I said again hurriedly.

Suddenly the man burst into laughter. "Oh, you mean Vallejo?" he asked, with the correct Spanish pronunciation.

I continued staring at him, unblinking, and he soon saw that I was in no laughing mood and quickly changed his attitude.

"Um…yes…just keep on heading north…you'll see signs." Needless to say it wasn't a very joyful trip back, but we all still got along and got the job done.

After 36 hours we finally got home to Missoula and it was a rush situation. I went right down to the railroad station. The army had already provided the means for me to go, but I didn't leave until the next day, so it gave me little over 24 hours to unpack and settle up everything as best I could. I had hoped to have the time to visit and compare notes with the others and talk to my folks and show them everything, but it was not to be. Our glorious six-week trip of nearly 9,000 miles had come to an end. It was all too brief of a farewell, and it was sad that we didn't get a chance to reminisce and talk it over. I think we all figured it was a once in a lifetime adventure in its own unique way, and we knew it was something that could never be repeated later on.

Though I had copied Bill in his idea of a Mexico trip, ours had been very different than his. Bill and his guys were more serious. Their goal had been more to go to ruins and museums and cultural places, but we didn't necessarily do those things. Our goal was much less defined. We had experienced life as it was, as simple as that.

Clark, me, and Ken: the end of a great adventure

Part 3:

Training

Hamming it up as a cadet – September 1942

It was tough departing for the army the day after the Mexico trip. Although it would have been nice to have more time in town with friends and family, I was still glad we were able to take such a long and adventurous trip in such times as they were. The freedom of the open road and the joy of exploring new places without much responsibility was a lifestyle that was quite different from what life in the army would be.

Full of anticipation, I hopped onto the train in Missoula to report to the aviation cadet center in San Antonio, Texas on September 16th, 1942. On board I was pleasantly surprised to meet two fellows from Spokane, Washington. Dick Rolfe was about my age and Virgil Solso was about three or four years older. The three of us already had something in common because they had also just completed their civilian pilot training in Spokane like I had in Missoula. Right away I enjoyed talking to Dick. He was very humorous and light-hearted and we hit it off immediately. Virg was a nice guy, but he wasn't quite the kids that Dick and I were.

The aviation cadet center was a huge new army facility near San Antonio and was split into two parts by the main road. On one side were the barracks for the incoming prospective cadets and the classification center, and on the other side was the actual cadet preflight training with lots of facilities for athletic training and ground school. This was all to prepare us for a future of flying.

Upon arrival we wore our civilian clothes and only carried a few brief toiletry articles with us. About a day or so later we lined up in the supply facility and were issued coveralls, shorts, underwear, and socks. We also received some G.I. (Government Issued) six-inch-high sturdy work shoes. And that was all we had to wear for a few days. They also supplied us with some toiletry articles, but I had already purchased a razor even though I had never shaved before. I figured I would probably be expected to shave my peach fuzz. I was still only nineteen but next month, on October 25th, I would be twenty years old. This was a benefit in a way because, as a young person, I was more malleable to learning things the army way and didn't have as many conflicts as the older cadets. For instance my brother Bill, being four years older, already had his personal habits fully formed and on his first day in training he extended his hand to give a friendly greeting to the upperclassmen. To his shock he was met in quite an unfriendly manner and they told him to pop to attention and promptly ignored his handshake. He thought that was rather ridiculous but when I arrived for training I was expecting it, and I was young and more care-free.

We didn't experience too much trouble with the upperclassmen at the classification center however, as it strictly focused on the business of getting us assigned to what they felt was a proper classification as an aviation cadet. There were three classifications: pilot, navigator, and bombardier. These were all positions that were in line for cadets to receive their gold bars and a commission as a second lieutenant, but a pilot was what nearly 90% of us wanted to become. A qualified army pilot received their silver wings after training, and this was our goal. Dick and I both thought it would be heaven if we were to get our gold bars and silver wings. We didn't worry much that we would be the peons, the lowest rank of the army officers, but we sure dreamed big. The next highest on the totem pole, in my judgment, were the navigators. They tended to be the brainy type, as being a navigator required considerable skill to be really proficient at it, and they were usually the first in math and other such subjects. The bombardiers were hard to label, but they tended to have more of the class clowns in their group. Their job focused strictly on weaponry and targeting and that classification was probably the least sought after. These, however, were just my thoughts and were often proved wrong.

Fortunately Dick, Virg, and I were all classified as pilots and were soon transferred across the road to preflight to start our training. We were assigned to a barracks where our closest associates were in the upper or lower bunk. The bunk I was assigned to was shared with a somewhat older cadet by the name of Simpson. By the time I got there he had already latched on to the lower bunk, and so I climbed up into the upper bunk with no problem. Dick and Virg were nearby, but still quite a few bunks away.

We were quick to adjust to army life. Waking up early in the morning, we would grab our towel and soap and whatever else was needed for a quick rise and shine and hurry to the latrines. There was no privacy, but that's just the way it was. Immediately the upperclassmen were on us and liked to rub it in that we were new. They had faced the same irritations as new cadets and now it was our turn. Typically we had to learn to make a bed precisely as the army directed and march in step in a military manner, and if we were out of line in the slightest the upperclassmen were on our case. The upperclassmen also had the authority to hand out punishment tasks called demerits. If something one of us had done was not up to their standard, they gave us a demerit. These were often worked off by walking back and forth on a ramp for an hour or doing a certain number of pushups.

I was glad for the ROTC experience I had received at Montana State University, as it put me at an advantage. I was also prepared for the tricks of the upperclassmen because I remember how Bill thought it was so arbitrary that he would have his bed or cupboard perfect, only to have them come along and mess it up and charge him demerits for it. That really bugged him. Dick and I, being younger and aware of the situation ahead of time, mostly had a hard time keeping a straight face when they chewed us out verbally for some made-up offense. So it was easier that way for me than it had been for Bill.

The rules were in every aspect in life, from the barracks and the latrines to the mess halls. While eating together we all had to sit very erect and ask for the food to be passed in a very polite and humble way, and failure to do so would earn more demerits. But the food was pretty good and I was pleased that we had quite a bit of milk to drink and ice cream and other desserts.

During physical training we did a great deal of cross-country running up and down little hills and other daily exercises early in the morning. The running soon gave us shin splints, which were rather painful, and soon it even hurt to walk around in training. There was no time to break-in your muscles or to get your muscles slowly in shape ahead of time. After we hardened up, however, it was kind of fun running across the Texas prairie and I did fairly well on pushups. Chin-ups were not so easy, but I was at least able to do the minimums without too much trouble. Needless to say, to soothe our sore muscles, the distinct odor of Sloan's Liniment was quite strong in the barracks for the first few weeks.

Throughout our cadet training we had a long day of activities and we got so we could drop off to sleep in any spare moment of free time. We were always ready to take a nap. Even a short sleep of ten to fifteen minutes was a blessing, and usually it really helped.

With time we adapted well to the system and a lot of our fellow cadets were pretty nice guys. After a couple weeks it was fun to look forward to an occasional pass to San Antonio. We would take an army bus in and pour out into the city. Dick, Virg and I were able to visit the Alamo and walk along the banks of the canals. Early on they said we had to go out and have a steak and a cocktail. It turned out they meant a shrimp cocktail, and to me as a Montana boy I didn't know what the heck a shrimp cocktail was, but I soon learned and thought it was very good. My world was expanding every day.

The first payday was a real pleasant surprise. The cadets lined up at a table and a sergeant gave you your pay for the month. The sergeant received a statement of any bills that we had incurred such as accommodation and laundry, and once that was all summarized it was subtracted from the full month's pay of 75 dollars. This was unlike the enlisted men who only got 21 dollars a month, although they didn't have to pay for accommodations. But on the first payday Dick and I were both pleased to find that we had accrued money as a private in the army reserve right from the moment we signed up. In my case this was May 25th, so the sergeant laid out several 20 dollar bills and I was really quite happy about that.

When we completed our course in preflight at San Antonio, Dick, Virg and I were among those assigned to primary flight school at Pine Bluff, Arkansas. The primary schools had a contract with the army to teach basic flying according to the standards set by the army. This meant we were no longer at an army base, but at a civilian school.

Pine Bluff was a small town and the percentage of black residents was probably half of the population, which was a new experience for me, again being a Montana boy. It was now December and there was snow on the ground, which was quite the switch from

Texas as the temperatures were often around freezing. Our assigned airplane was the Fairchild Primary Trainer (PT)-19. It was a low-wing monoplane with a fixed landing gear and an open cockpit. We were issued heavy flying clothes that were leather and lined with sheepskin for warmth.

We were to train here for a nine-week period, and our training included a more intensive ground school on some of the things I'd learned in civilian pilot training such as weather, flying regulations, radio code, and other allied subjects. I certainly felt better already having my 40 hours with a Piper Cub. It gave me considerable more confidence, but I knew I was going to have to be on the ball to make it through training anyway. Nearly a third of the cadets typically washed out during training, so I was very eager to do well and complete it.

My instructor was a very friendly civilian pilot named Mr. Wright. He was very capable and quiet-spoken, and it was a pleasure having him as my instructor. He also thought I had pretty good basic knowledge for an incoming cadet, which I was glad to hear, as it took the pressure off a little bit. When I had flown only four hours, my instructor said he thought I could solo, even though the minimum requirement was at eight hours. He was apparently more confident in me than I was in myself. When I did solo at the required eight hours we flew around together first and then I made a landing or two for him. He got out and waved me on and I took off by myself this time and started to circle the field. During my

Sheepskin lined suit to combat the cold

landing I wasn't feeling that confident and it seemed like I was coming in at a little higher speed than I wanted to, and I didn't feel like I had the airplane fully in my grasp to slow down. But somehow it worked anyway and I landed successfully. From there on we progressed gradually. Some of the new things we learned were flying in precise patterns over the ground and being able to recover from a stall. Those were always intense because you're no longer in control after a stall, so learning how to recover was important.

I wrote to my folks about my training and one of the pleasures of my limited down time was to go down to the Post Exchange. There we could mail letters and buy all kinds of items and could have whatever we wanted to eat or drink. I was quite taken with having a sundae with candied mixed fruit on top of my vanilla ice cream. I thought that was quite yummy. And of course we had spending money and could buy souvenirs or whatever to send home to a girlfriend. I, of course, didn't have one, but I enjoyed the thought all the same.

While I was experiencing the little ups and downs of training, the war across the ocean was raging on. Close to the end of my flying time in primary I received news from my mother that my brother Bill, fighting in North Africa, had been reported missing in action. This was a severe blow to me, but I was on such a hectic schedule that I had little time to grieve, which was maybe for the better, as it wouldn't be the last bad news I'd hear while in training.

Dick, Virg and I graduated primary school on schedule and moved on to basic training. The location was Winfield, Kansas, a small town near the Arkansas border in the southeastern part of the state. It was March when we arrived and it was cold, windy, and quite often cloudy. We were in barracks with probably twenty cadets per barrack. The building was heated with coal by a fairly large round stove in the center of the room. In the early morning we would be awakened by the orderly coming in, who would shake the grates and load in more coal and stomp out of the barracks. It was cold and smoky quite a bit of the time and that put a bit of a damper on things as well.

Basic training was essentially a whole new story. We no longer had a nice personable civilian instructor, but either an army first or second lieutenant who wanted to make sure you realized you were back in the army. Things were going to be much stricter and more rigid than we had had it at Pine Bluff.

I was kind of leery about how well I'd do with the Vultee Basic Training (BT)-13 aircraft. It was a lot more of an airplane than the primary airplane, bigger and more powerful, and I knew I had to be fully alert to master it if I wanted to graduate. It did have sturdy, wide-track landing gear, which was good for beginners. My instructor was a first lieutenant by the name of Dench. He seemed to be fairly content with my flying and didn't chew me out or get after me. There was one cadet he picked on, though. Dench thought he was way too cocky and flippant so he proceeded to work him over. One time he made the poor cadet write on the blackboard about twenty or thirty times: *I am sh** on the stick.* I thought, now that's kind of crude, and after that in my own mind I called him Stinky Dench, but I was careful not to say it out loud, of course.

During one of his ground lessons he asked all of us, there were four or five of us in his group, to write a few paragraphs of our life to date. I did this the best I could and I mentioned my brother Bill being an idol for me. His wife read that and Dench said his wife wanted to meet me because she really liked my little story. She came down the flight line one time and I was introduced to her, but I guess I wasn't very impressive because it was a very brief meeting and that's the last I heard of it. I don't know if she imagined me to be a Don Juan or some other literary genius, but she hardly said boo and I hardly said boo, so I guess she was quite disappointed.

Continuing with my training I tried to be on my best behavior and went along and soloed at about an average length of time. My first trouble occurred when I was on a solo flight in the area. I was slotted for a one hour flight, so I had a lot of time to practice my maneuvers, such as trying to do a little bit of flight aligned with the ground.

When I came back to land the tower announced, "All aircraft do not land. There has been an accident on the runway. Do not land."

So, like the rest of the planes, I circled around for a little while and when it was clear for landing again there was a buildup of several aircraft. Before my turn came around there was another announcement.

"We are changing runways due to a shift in wind direction," the tower said. "Do not land."

Circling back around to the other runway, I was finally able to land, but was well over my allotted hour of flight time. I hadn't announced my arrival until that final landing, and when I landed I was met with Captain Austin, the director of flight training.

"I've never seen such a stupid action!" he started, and he continued to chew me out for what he assumed was a pleasure ride, where I had just ridden around the country willy-nilly.

I was baffled, I didn't know why he hadn't understood that I had been delayed by the tower, but I didn't say anything. I didn't offer the excuse of the change of runways involved, and I was supposed to only say, and only did say, "Yes, sir. No, sir. No excuse, sir."

Later it finally dawned on me why Captain Austin hadn't understood. I had forgotten to change my radio frequency from the tower's to the frequency of those who were flying in the area. There had been no announcements from the tower, but they had been looking for me on the other frequency. After realizing this I thought for a moment that I should find him and tell him, but, timid me, I did not. So I was in the dog house with Captain Austin and he proceeded to levy a fairly steep punishment in the form of demerits that had to be worked off on the ramp marching back and forth with a rifle. I had earned ten hours of this from him to work off, and it also meant I couldn't have any leave time until it was taken care of. It was a bit of a bummer because my buddy Dick Rolfe was able to go to town on brief trips and I was stuck at the base.

That was not to be the end of my problems at basic. Coming back to land from another solo flight, I knew that I was too high, but I didn't want to go around and try another landing, thus disregarding any of the training I'd learned so far. I decided that since this plane was a lot heavier than the primary plane, if I cut the throttle it would settle down and would reach the desired altitude for a proper landing. I didn't just ease off the throttle because I wanted to get down quickly, so I chopped it off.

Immediately the right wing dropped down 90 degrees, pointing directly at the ground. I was stunned. My reaction was; this is a disaster, I'm going to crash. I was headed for the ground in a deadly manner, and rapidly.

Out of the blue a voice said to me, *do something!* In a matter of split seconds I popped the stick forward and hit the throttle. The plane righted itself just in time and I made a perfect landing toward the end of the runway.

The tower said immediately, "Cadet Schottelkorb, report to your squadron commander."

Guess who that was, it was Captain Austin. I didn't reply and sank a little lower in my seat. It wasn't far to the ramp but he was already there when I taxied up, looking erect and polished in his uniform. Dazed, I shut off my engine and sat there. I didn't say anything or attempt to get out. I knew if I got out my knees would be knocking together. So I just sat there and looked straight ahead. Captain Austin immediately went around the airplane and looked it over closely. Not finding anything wrong he went around a second time, this time putting his hand under the edge of the wing tip to see if I had scraped the runway. Completing his second loop he came around and gave me a good, hard look. He didn't say a word, and I didn't say a word, and that was a small miracle in my mind. I also didn't say anything to my instructor when I saw him, and he never said anything to me. It had to have been a perfect landing, because there was no room for error in those few seconds.

"You bragging, saying you landed that perfectly?" my friends asked me later as I told my story.

"No way, man, I wasn't flying then," I said. I was just a lowly cadet. "I wasn't flying that plane. My guardian angel was flying that plane."

With time I did start to improve. On one occasion I had a buddy ride with a fellow cadet. He was assigned to the front seat and I to the rear cockpit seat. He was in charge as the pilot, and we had just taken off when the engine started to sputter and wasn't getting full power. Immediately he turned around and gave me a panicked look.

This time I knew the answer and I said, "Turn on the carburetor heat!"

It was obvious that the carburetor was icing up in the cold temperatures, it was the right condition for that. The engine responded straightaway and was back to normal. I felt a little smug, but neither of us said anything about it when we got back. I should have called the tower and reported the icing and the problem encountered, but I didn't. I might have made some brownie points for myself and, of course, it could have prevented an accident by some other cadet.

All in all it seemed like basic wasn't too much fun and I was still worried if I was going to be able to pass the required tests to continue my flying in a positive manner. One thing that especially worried me was that cadets had to pass flight checks after a certain number of hours. When my turn came around the person who I was going to fly with was a first lieutenant, a big, raw-boned, stern-looking man. He had me feeling rather subdued when I had to report to him for my check flight. I really didn't feel like trying to butter him up or anything, I just wanted to do what I had to, and soon we were taking off.

One of the big tests was successfully pulling out of a stall and spin. Again though, this plane was much bigger and heavier than the PT-19 I had flown, which made it more violent. When I got up to sufficient altitude I pulled the stick clear back and held it, cutting the throttle and forcing the plane into a deliberate stall. The plane immediately dropped down and headed down toward the ground. We started spinning and every time the plane completed a 360 degree spin it would vibrate violently, shaking the whole plane, and I learned why its nickname was the 'Vultee Vibrator.' During the forceful spin I knew damn well I needed to make a fully-fledged recovery and not mince around. So after I was told to recover the plane I popped the stick forward, gave it full throttle, and made a decent recovery, leveling out in a positive manner. The lieutenant also made me do a series of turns and so forth, which I also felt fine about, but as we were returning to the airfield he suddenly grabbed the stick, whipped it back and forth, and kicked the rudders rather violently. I wondered what in the hell he was trying to tell me, but, true to my form, I didn't ask him what I was doing wrong. Later on I thought that maybe it was just his way of saying loosen up. During the flight, though, I just sat in silence, thinking that he was going to give me a terrible grade and that I wouldn't pass the test. Full of anxiety, we landed, I shut the engine off, and he never said anything. He simply walked away. Quite depressed, I wrote my folks right away and said I was afraid I had failed the check flight and was going to wash out.

When I talked to my instructor Dench the next day I asked him, "How did I do, sir?"

"Well," he said, "the worst thing you did was you shut the ignition off before you shut off the fuel switch."

This meant it was possible there was some unspent fuel in the line and if somebody was near the propeller when the switch was turned on it could turn the prop over before anybody expected it. Dench didn't say anything else before walking off, which was perhaps an awkward way to say I'd done pretty well. I was still nervous until later on when I officially learned that I had indeed passed.

We learned to fly solo at night and that was a new feeling of success. Bill had written letters rather eloquently about his flying, especially in basic. When he learned night flying and went up on a clear night he thought it was just gorgeous. It was rather impressive all right, but I didn't really make such a nice story out of it in my own letters home as he had. It was satisfying though to be able to make a night solo flight and bring the plane back successfully and mission completed.

Before we completed our course in basic flying we were asked to fill out a questionnaire on what type of a plane we would want to fly when we finished our cadet training. We had a choice between single-engine aircraft, more quick and agile, or the bigger, multi-engine aircraft. We had only been exposed to very minimal acrobatic maneuvers and when I briefly tried to perform the ones we had been shown I didn't think I did very well. I wasn't very adept at those and also at the time a B-24, a four-engine bomber, had landed at the airfield and I thought, boy, if I could fly that baby, I'd be king! So in the questionnaire I put multi-engine. My friend Dick Rolfe, I called him a natural hot pilot, put in for single-engine and when we graduated he was assigned to Mission, Texas near the gulf coast in hot, humid country, whereas I was assigned to Altus, Oklahoma, which was for multi-engine training. There was not a ceremony when we graduated from basic, and it was kind of sad that Dick and I were split off and sent to different air bases. We still kept in touch occasionally by letter, but that was the last time I saw him. In the meantime, Virgil Solso was washed out of the class and failed to advance to further training, which meant he would be assigned to some other non-flying duty and reduced in rank. In both classes at primary and basic I believe the attrition rate was close to thirty percent, so I thank my lucky stars that I was able to continue on. Virgil did marry his girlfriend in Spokane, who was the daughter of a doctor there. It was Virg's dream to marry her, so that part of his life was a plus and according to plan.

Altus, Oklahoma was a small town. As I remember it, the center of town had a public square and everything radiated out from there. I never really made it into town much and I usually stayed at the base. Although I still made errors from time to time, there wasn't much of a chance of washing out. We were no longer pestered by the upperclassmen, so that was nice. It was kind of a given that if you made it through basic you pretty well had it made unless you goofed up majorly. They had spent enough time with you already and they didn't want to wash you out for a minor infraction or flying error.

The advanced trainer airplane was a fairly easy transition from the basic trainer in the air. It was a Cessna AT-17 Bobcat and had the nickname 'Double-breasted Cub' because of its relatively low horsepower twin engines. It was more powerful, of course, but similar to the low horsepower of the Piper Cub I had flown in civilian training. It didn't have any particularly dangerous features, but it took a little getting used to manipulating the two throttles so that when taxiing or running up the power to both engines I could do it evenly and not zig-zag along the flight line. I do remember it was fun flying near the fluffy white cumulous clouds on a sunny afternoon.

My flying partner and I took turns alternating who would be the pilot and copilot. I never did become very close with any of the cadets there so it was a little lonely in a way, especially since I had parted with my friend Dick and was still dealing with the news that my brother was missing in action, which meant he was captured or dead. To make matters worse, in May I received a letter from my mother stating that my close friend Ken Rigby had drowned in a boating accident in the Clark Fork River just east of Missoula. This came as a terrible shock and I could not understand it. It happened just as the university let out for summer break, the 30th of May. I'm glad she wrote a letter instead of calling, because it would have been too emotional for me to deal with.

Ken had drowned when the height of the river was at its highest and swiftest. For some reason Ken and another student at the university decided to try floating with a kayak from the Milltown Dam a few miles east of Missoula into town as a fitting celebration for the school break. True to form, Ken was dressed in his usual nice street clothes and had strapped on his 22-revolver. Why he needed that I don't know, he just wanted to do it up proud I guess, but at any rate it wasn't long before the boat began to leak at a recent patch he had put on and by the time they got close to Missoula it was leaking badly and starting to sink. Ken and his friend jumped out and started swimming, but Ken was still not much of a swimmer. He took a few strokes and sank from sight in a rush of water. The friend made it to the shore and pulled himself up onto the bank and reported it immediately, but it was too late.

His body wasn't recovered until August. It was badly decomposed and washed up on a small island just west of Missoula. I received a telegram from the Missoula authorities asking me if I could identify the revolver he had. Of course, it was a matching revolver to my nine-shot H&R 22, so that served to confirm that it was indeed Ken's body. His parents and friends were shocked, it was a time of war, but Ken hadn't been a part of that at all. It was a tragic end for such a close friend, someone who had been such a big part of my life. Maybe it was fortunate that I was so busy with my training that I didn't have too much time to sit around and dwell on it. I was keenly aware of the loss, but my busy schedule kept me on track.

When it came time to graduate there was a very brief ceremony where we received our gold bars to signify we were now second lieutenants and our silver wings as pilots. A lot had happened since my friend Dick and I had dreamed of this day back at the classification center in San Antonio. Normally one of the parents or a girlfriend would pin the bars and wings on, but I had neither at the ceremony. A fellow cadet and I took care of this for each other and our class was designated 43-F. It was the 26th of June 1943 and I was ready to move on to a new place. We were all assigned to airfields in various locations, and my orders were to report only a few days later to Liberal, Kansas.

Before coming to Liberal I had indicated on a questionnaire that I would like to do any further training in the northwest United States, where I was from. The closest I got to that was Liberal, Kansas, out among the level wheat fields of southwest Kansas close to the border with Oklahoma. Liberal was not a very exciting town. True, they didn't have any mountains to crash into, but I didn't think there was much to see or do on off-duty hours. So I wasn't too wild about the town itself, but it was pretty good for flying. The field had nice long runways and it was fairly new. There were duel runways on the main ones where two planes could land side by side if the occasion called for it. The field also had a nice Post Exchange where you could buy clothing or other items as well as two or three food outlets. The officers' club, which I was now a member of, had a nice swimming pool and I ate, of course, in the officer's mess hall. The food was pretty good, and every Friday it was often fish. Sometimes I lingered there and I took the little pieces of lemon wedges and squeezed them into my ice water, and that was a nice little treat of lemonade.

I did gradually become acquainted with a few of my fellow officers. The one that I liked the best, and seemed to be the best fit for a friend, was a quiet-spoken, rather tancomplexioned guy of Italian decent named Salvadore 'Sal' Mauriello. I didn't call him by his first name because it sounded kind of girlish, so I called him Maury. Anyway, we were able to pal around a little bit and it was soon evident that he was quite the ladies' man. He had a nice build and a pleasant manner.

One day he gave me a little advice and said, "When you're out in town don't ever be too anxious to cross the street. Linger a little bit and look around and see if you might see some gal that might look interesting. If so, slowly saunter in her direction if it's convenient."

I never followed that information when I was alone, but it was fun hearing his occasional bits of advice.

With Maury at the officers' club swimming pool

Going from a little twin-engine trainer to the B-24 was quite a jump. Complete with four engines, it was a big airplane. If the engines were running, people could enter and exit through the small back door just forward of the tail section, though usually we would duck under the open bomb bay doors, a series of metals slats that conformed to the contour of the fuselage, to enter onto the deck. From there it was possible to climb up into the cockpit area. This was dangerous, as you always had to stay aware of the spinning propellers.

At first the cockpit seemed like a maze of instruments, but, like all things, with gradual steps and under the supervision of a flight instructor it slowly became a little easier. One of the early things that bothered me was mastering the four throttles. They stuck in the control module straight up and you had to put your hands on top and learn to manipulate the individual throttles. My instructor said I was as clumsy as a bear cub, which was probably accurate, but I didn't appreciate the remark.

Being in control of a large plane, I also had to be careful simply when taxiing to make sure I stayed on the narrow taxiways. One time my instructor was letting me taxi through an area where they had been doing a little excavation work adjacent to the taxiway, when I managed to slip off the pavement. The instructor was a little irritated with me, I could tell, but he hadn't caught me in time to avert that little incident. It wasn't anything serious but there was a small hump of dirt obstructing the right wheel so we couldn't move forward. I cut back on the throttles, my instructor jumped out, and I followed him. The engines were still running and he started to kick at the small mound of dirt. It wasn't very big, but he was a bit put out and kicking hard, and without realizing it he swung his arm close to the idling propellers and got a blow to his arm.

The engineer along with us was watching all this and he was right there when it happened. Grabbing the instructor, he pulled him back as I jumped back in the B-24 and radioed the tower of an emergency. Frantically I looked around for a first aid kit. I was sure I had seen it just behind the cockpit, but when I looked it wasn't there. The different aircraft models put things in different places, and I couldn't find it. Frustrated, I jumped back out to see if I could do anything without one. However, the engineer had everything taken care of. He had wisely pulled off his belt and improvised with a tourniquet on the instructor's arm. There was a deep cut across it, but it definitely could have been worse. Soon an ambulance took him away and a new instructor was sent out to get me corralled. I never had any repercussions for the incident. It truly had been an accident after all. After that I was always thankful to have a good engineer on board, especially once I got my own crew.

Taxiing on the ground in the B-24 was tricky enough, but flying it was somewhat challenging. In the air it was very heavy on the controls, as there was no power assist. Later in the program we started night flying and were assigned to evening training. There were often thunderstorms in the evenings, and that always made me feel on edge. Waiting around in the operations room for my turn to fly, I hated seeing the lightning flash around us. I had a habit of pacing around the floor when I got nervous, and I did a lot of yawning to try and relieve my anxiety. But actually accidents from aircraft being struck by lightning and resulting in a crash were pretty rare, usually it wasn't too serious and the high voltage would dissipate off the airplane. It all still made me nervous nonetheless.

Accidents were frequent in other areas, however, and while I was training in Liberal there were two crashes shortly after takeoff when the B-24 just exploded and burst into flame. It was assumed that static electricity had possibly ignited gasoline leaking from the aircraft, and that wasn't good news. We heard about more crashes through the newspaper. Frequently the B-26 twin-engine medium bomber was in the reports, mostly from an airbase at Dodge City, Kansas, about 50 miles north of Liberal. There was apparently a flaw in the engine design which would cause the engine to shut down suddenly, causing all sorts of problems. But life goes on and we kept climbing in our airplanes to train.

At about this time a fellow lieutenant in my class gave me a poem about Liberal and the B-24. It was a poem called "The Unsung Hero's Lament", and it poked fun at the quality of the B-24 and flying at Liberal, Kansas. The Lieutenant's name was R.J. Smith. I didn't know him very well, but we met up a time or two and one time he wanted me to take a swig out of his pint bottle of whiskey. That didn't appeal to me so I turned him down but he persisted and pressured me to go ahead and take it. I finally did so and, of course, no doubt made quite a face, but that seemed to satisfy him and that's about all the conversation we really had. The poem he gave me though was quite humorous, talking about Kansas as "the land that God forgot" and the B-24 as quite a run-down piece of machinery, despite the fact that "for those who land, and still can stand, fly the goddam thing tomorrow." I realized that a die-hard B-24 pilot would take exception to that type of humor and perhaps the airbase in Liberal didn't care for it either. And besides, we B-24 pilots did not want the B-17 pilots to feel superior. Nevertheless, the humor in the poem made me chuckle.

-    The Unsung Hero's Lament   -

They sat in state, the heroes in the vaulted Halls of Fame,
In proud and scornful silence, for each had made his name
On fields of storied battle, on many a bloody sea,
Though forged in fire, or carved in mire, each deed is history.

There was little Davy Crockett, and the martyr, Nathan Hale,
And that rebel line that fell in Shenandoah's bloody dale,
There was Grant, who knew brief glory, but died another way,
And others known to time alone, but each had had his day.

There was on each haunted visage, a deep, forbidding gloom,
And every gaze upon a stranger who had shambled into the room.
In his left hand was a check list, in his right an R.B.I.
His face was worn, his clothes were torn, his flight cap was awry.

The first to speak was Ceasar, by virtue of his age,
And the finger that he pointed was trembling with his rage,
"What right have ye brash youngster, with these gallant men of yore?"
And the man replied, though not with pride, "I flew a B-24."

"It was out on the plains of Kansas, in the land that God forgot.
Where the winter winds are piercing, and the summer suns are hot.
We were young and brave and hopeful, fresh from ten day leaves,
Though somehow we knew, and the feeling grew, they were really last reprieves.

For there's a sort of maniac madness in the supercharger's whine,
As you hear the ice cubes tinkling in the Turbo Balance Line,
And the runway strips are narrow, but the snowbanks they were wide;
While the crash trucks say, in a mournful way, that you're on your final ride.

The nose gear rocks and trembles, for it's held with bailing wire,
And the wings are filled with thermite to make a hotter fire.
The camouflage is peeling off, it lends an added luster,
While the pitot head is filled with lead to help the load adjuster.

The bomb bay doors are rusted, and they close with a ghastly shriek,
And the plexiglass is smeared from some forgotten leak.
The oleo struts are twisted, the wheels are not quite round,
And the bulkheads thin, admit the slightest sound.

Your taxi out to the runway, 'mid the groans of the tortured gear,
And you feel the check rider's practiced teeth, gnawing on your tender rear,
The co-pilot dozing on the right, in a liquor laden coma,
Mingles his breath, like the kiss of death, with the put-put's foul aroma.

So it's off in the overcast younger, though number one is missing,
And the hydraulic fluid escaping, sets up a gentle hissing.
The compass dial is spinning in a way that broods no stopping,
And row by row, the fuses blow with an intermittent popping.

It was named the "LIBERATOR" by a low and twisted mind,
But the men who come to Liberal, no freedom ever find;
There is no hope, no sunny ray, to dry their tears of sorrow,
For those who land, and still can stand, fly the goddam thing tomorrow."

The stranger's voice was silent, a tear shone in his eye,
And from all his honored audience arose a vastly sigh,
Great Ceasar rose up to him with pity on his face
And bowing low, he turned to show the stranger to his place.

Many years later I learned the name of the author. His name was Lieutenant L.W. Coquillette and had been at Liberal around the same time as me. I thought he was pretty clever.

I'd just finished my nine-week B-24 training in September of 1943 and my new assignment was to be an instructor pilot. That was not to my liking. I did not want to be an instructor in B-24s. For one thing they were hard to maneuver and heavy on the controls, and if a trainee got me in a bad position while he was in charge it might be difficult to recover and cause an accident. I also didn't have any previous instructor training, but before long I learned that this was just a very temporary assignment for the convenience of the army. They planned to ship me out later when they had accumulated a large enough group to send on to further specialized combat training.

To my surprise, who should show up also as an instructor, but the first lieutenant who had intimidated me back in basic when I was on a check ride with him. Back then he had kicked the rudders and startled me without saying a word. I thought I was going to be washed out. I had a nickname for him then, I won't repeat it, but he was rather intimidating. He was rugged looking and pretty good sized. He was an ideal B-24 pilot because he was able to handle the heavy controls without much of a problem.

When we bumped in to each other in the operations room we were both surprised and he came over and shook my hand and said, "Oh yeah, Schottelkorb. Good boy!"

Of course, I didn't ask him about my check ride from basic and the trouble he had given me. I guess he would have just laughed and said that I was a scared little cadet back then. That's the last time I ran into him.

So even though I knew it wouldn't last long, it was my job at the moment and I was assigned to instruct these two lieutenants. I was certainly lacking in experience and expertise, as I only had about four and a half weeks more training than they did, so training them was a bit awkward to begin with. We focused a lot on instrument flying. This involved one student sitting in the pilot seat screened behind a little curtain so they couldn't see outside, and then I had to try and instruct them on the instruments. On one of our flights, after an hour and a half or so of flying around, I decided we'd better head back to the base. The only problem was we didn't know where we were. I didn't have a clue. I was so busy talking to the students and trying to keep an eye out to avoid any possible collisions with other aircraft that I had completely lost track of where we were and they didn't know either. We'd been told to be back by one o-clock, but we were out in flat country, wheat ranches and farms everywhere, so I wasn't too sure we'd make our deadline.

Most of the towns, however, got their water from wells. They pumped the water up into towers and distributed the water with gravity through the town's piping system. Usually the name of the town was painted onto the side of the water tower, just like a big sign. Decreasing our altitude to read the signs, we got down quite low and swooped over a town. The problem was we were still too fast and it was too hard to read the town name. It was kind of ridiculous, but that was the case. We wandered around for some time trying to get a good take on it, but none of us could seem to come up with a name for quite a while. When we finally made it back, I reported late. Nobody said anything, but there was supposed to have been a meeting at that time, so I missed that. Later I thought, well, why in the world didn't I ask the sergeant (the engineer) who was riding with us? But being a fresh young second lieutenant I didn't think of that solution. He was probably sitting back laughing. You live and learn.

One perk of being an instructor was that I did get to take a few cross-country trips. During one trip I was with two senior pilot instructors, one acting as co-pilot. The other pilot was serving as an observer on this trip, which meant I was able to fly as pilot. Our destination was New York City and the small army air force field called Floyd Bennett Field on Long Island. I made a good approach and felt very much in control and had a good landing, but as soon as I got on the runway, the senior pilot instructor stood up behind me and started yelling,

"Get on the brakes! Get on the brakes!" Apparently he felt we were coming in too fast and he wanted to be sure we could turn off at the designated taxiway.

I, however, felt that things were well under control and didn't make any changes. I didn't say anything, per usual, and I just continued as I had planned. It was a very satisfactory roll to the flight line and there were no further complaints from the senior officers.

We toured around New York City for the remainder of that afternoon, and in the evening we got a room in the Hotel Astor on Time's Square. The room was $4.50, and since we were two to a room I paid half of it. Who can beat two and a quarter! It was the first time I had ever been in New York and it was rather impressive for a small town boy.

Later on our return trip, with me still in the pilot seat, we headed into an area of thunderheads, complete with lightning and downdraft winds. We were flying along and all of the sudden our plane was lifted up rapidly, straight up with little or no control on my part. Then, without warning, we were dragged into the downdraft and started immediately plunging toward earth. Frankly, it scared the hell out of me because I'd never experienced a wind shear before. I did as instructed by the senior pilot this time, and he told me to lower the landing gear when I was going up in an updraft and then to retract them when we were being forced down. This was a very awkward and slow procedure. I couldn't see that it accomplished anything, but I was really under duress, we all were. I doubted that it was an approved procedure, but I did as I was instructed. Finally we flew out of that area, thankfully with all of our feathers intact.

One of the biggest blessings during my time at Liberal was when I learned that one instructor wanted to go to Spokane, Washington overnight and, since I was also an instructor and allowed a few cross-country trips, he agreed to drop me off in my hometown of Missoula, Montana. That enabled me to make my first trip home since my induction in September 1942, as it was now early October of 1943. Flying this time as a passenger, I elected not to call my parents to notify them of my plans. We landed at Missoula County Airport, I called a taxi, and pulled up to our house on Blaine Street. Mom said my dog Shep let out a certain yelp when I got out and she knew that meant me, and that I had arrived. It was a joyful reunion for Mom, Shep and I. Mom then called Dad at work and he was able to get off a little early for lunch and had the rest of the day off. It was pretty profound being back. I had been quite homesick when I was first in the army, and although the fellowship of friends I'd met helped relieve that, it was nice being in familiar territory again, even if just overnight.

When the orders finally came for me to report at the airbase Hill Field near Salt Lake City, I found out that my good friend Jay Lockhart's name was also on the list of those with the same orders as me. I hadn't seen him since civilian pilot training at the university, but he had apparently started at Liberal four and a half weeks after I did. Jay had been delayed at the cadet center in San Antonio because of medical issues. They checked out a heart murmur which was eventually resolved, and now since I had been stalled for a few weeks at Liberal as an instructor pilot we were entering the next phase together.

Pleasantly surprised to be together again, we were also allowed a ten-day leave before reporting to Salt Lake City, and it coincided with my birthday in October, the 25th. So Jay and I both were back in Missoula and had a pleasant time off. In fact we were enjoying it so much we wired the authorities to ask for an extension, but that was promptly returned with a negative reply saying we were to report as previously ordered.

On leave with Jay Lockhart

When we arrived back in Salt Lake City, we still had a weekend off before we had to officially report. Jay met up with a buddy he flew with named Jeff and the three of us wanted to do something that first evening. They had the idea of calling a nurse's training hospital to see if there were any trainees willing to go out with some young lieutenants. There didn't seem to be any problem with that, and we ended up with three nice young ladies. We talked a bit with them and decided it would be good to go to a dance hall. Here again I thought, oh boy, I can't dance.

I went along anyway with the others, and upon arrival I said to the nice young gal I was accompanying, "I'm sorry. I can't dance."

"That's ok," she said with a smile, and was very nice about it. She wore glasses and had a very nice personality. We got along fine and chatted a while.

In the meantime Jay's buddy, Jeff, excused himself and was gone only a short period of time. When he came back he had two pint bottles of whiskey. So when we ordered a soft drink we all poured a little tonic into our glasses. I hadn't done much socializing since the start of my training, so I figured it could be fun.

After about two drinks I turned to my gal, feeling confident. "I believe I can dance," I said.

And with that we got up and proceeded to do a reasonable dance and she sort of rolled her eyes at me as if saying, why did you wait so long? So we had an enjoyable evening. The only downside of it was that the girl Jeff was with became quite sick, so that eliminated any romantic inclination for him, but overall it was a pleasant evening and I had learned a cure for my shyness.

In Salt Lake City we received our combat training assignments. This was a three stage process and the first part of my training was at Davis-Monthan in Tucson, Arizona. Jay was assigned elsewhere, and that was the last I saw of him before the end of the war. Tucson appeared to be a nice city and the temperature was pleasant when I arrived in November. In my first crew I was assigned as the co-pilot. The pilot was an army captain who had previously flown with the Royal Canadian Air Force. I was a little disappointed at being just a co-pilot, but this army captain no doubt had a lot of experience, and I figured I could learn something from him.

Only a week or so later I was replaced by a first lieutenant, a buddy of the captain, who had also been in the RCAF, and so I got to be the pilot of the crew he left. I was pleased to be the pilot, but it also meant that if I was going to continue with the class, our crew had to do some extra flying together to catch me up with the training that I had missed while I was a co-pilot. So I never did see much of Tucson, but I was pleased to have my own crew, and it was an entirely new experience for me learning to be part of a team.

In time I got well acquainted with the crew members. Four of us were second lieutenants and Charlie was perhaps my favorite companion. He was the valued navigator of the crew. The oldest of the group, he would have loved to have been a pilot, but his eyes weren't good enough to operate a powered aircraft. My co-pilot, E.L. Wager, was a guy that was probably not too happy about being a co-pilot, but he seemed qualified for his duties. He also liked to drink pretty well. Early on I was impressed with the bombardier, Del Ladwig. He appeared to be a quiet, sincere person, and he was quite easy to talk with, and it turned out he was also very well qualified and very good at his job.

Six enlisted men were also in the crew, they were all sergeants. The engineer was perhaps the most important because he was trained in mechanics and he was the one who watched over things and saw if they weren't working properly. For instance if the landing gear failed to respond to the switch, they could be lowered by the engineer or someone manually cranking the wheels down and locking them in position. He was also ranked higher than the others and was staff sergeant.

The other enlisted men in the crew were the gunners, and now that we were in combat training they got a lot of practice. We had one gunner, Kirk, who was assigned one of the two waist gunner positions, one for each side of the plane. His job was to fire a .50 caliber machine gun on a swivel out the windows on each side of the rear fuselage. The air could be pretty rough in the afternoons, and the rear of the aircraft was worse for swinging back and forth in the unstable air. Kirk got airsick quite frequently, and he would throw up into an empty container of the spent ammunition belts. One of the other gunners remarked to me that he didn't know about Kirk because when he looked in the can there were quite large chunks of un-chewed sausages. He thought, boy, Kirk really wolfs them down! But unfortunately he also lost them just as quickly.

All of the crew members did a good deal of sizing each other up during our training. I wanted to be sure I was a decent pilot for them so I worked hard to be at my best. In the end we all seemed to be a good fit for each other, and it was on to further training.

The time in Tucson passed quickly and it was around Christmas when our crew was assigned to Biggs Field in El Paso, Texas for the second and third phase of combat training. We were right in west Texas and just across the border from Juárez, Mexico. That town was a bit crazy. There was the occasional murder or stabbing, and then the army had to cancel passes into town, making it off-limits for a while, but then things would get better, and we could go back and visit.

We welcomed in the New Year with a night flight, as a six man crew. It was an instrument flight, and we tried to find the Alamogordo bombing range in New Mexico but failed to do so. Upon our return, we learned that one B-24 didn't return from a night flight. They looked for it for days. It was beautiful to see the lights of a city appear out of the black night, but it could also be quite scary out in the dark if you were lost. This was one of many crashes that occurred during our training. The next evening we made it to Alamogordo with a bombardier instructor and, at the range, Del dropped ten bombs with very good results. The instructor said it was excellent work and that Del was the best bombardier he had ever ridden with. It soon became apparent that we were going to do a lot more cross-country flights than in previous training, and that could be interesting. Things were starting to move at a much faster pace.

January 1ˢᵗ, 1944

This year I decided to start a diary as it should be a pretty eventful year; probably will be in combat a few months from now.

The following day we got up at 04:30 to be ready for a 05:30 briefing. The mission: a six-ship formation flight with air-to-air gunnery firing at a target pulled by a twin-engine B-26 bomber. It was a worthwhile mission but very tiring, six hours long. The B-24s are just plain work flying formation. During the flight the two gunners got sick. Kirk lost his false teeth as well as everything else in the ammunition box he threw up in. The other gunner got his lip smacked when the nose gun kicked back at him, apparently it wasn't properly locked in place. Needless to say, we were all ready for a good night's sleep when we got back.

January 12th, 1944

A B-24 crashed 35 miles north of the field and killed seven men and critically injured another this afternoon.

January 13th, 1944

Three engines conked out on a B-24 today, but all got out alive. All of the crew bailed out but the pilot who rode it down. He got minor scratches, etc. The plane burned. The co-pilot was last to jump (and a little low to do so) and he broke both of this ankles.

During our down time the crew all got along well. We officers went to shows quite often and went out for drinks now and then as well. Pranks were also a common theme and one time when Charlie was out on a date, the remaining trio, Del, E.L. and I, did some plotting. We 'short-sheeted' Charlie's bed, essentially making his bed so that the sheet turned back on itself halfway down instead extending the full length. This would make it quite difficult for him to get into bed, especially when stumbling around in the middle of the night. It was 'mission accomplished' upon his return.

January 16th, 1944

Slept late this morning. Ground school at the theatre only lasted an hour, but it broke up the afternoon. Otherwise had the whole day off.

Spent most of the evening reading an accumulation of Sentinels, my hometown newspaper. Fortunately we don't have to get up at 04:30.

After we'd been training a couple of weeks, Charlie, E.L. and I went over to Juárez for a Saturday night celebration. We wanted to go to a nice restaurant and have a steak dinner along with drinks. Charlie by this time had introduced me to the frozen daiquiri. I hadn't done much drinking and I didn't care for beer at that point, and so I was to start my drinking with frozen daiquiris. Sipping away on my daiquiri, we had been there some time when Charlie got up to go to the restroom. When he came back his foot loudly kicked a brass spittoon, which he hadn't seen on the floor. Clanking and rattling across the floor as it rolled away, Charlie hurriedly sat down and tried to avoid the eyes of everyone in the restaurant. This was rather embarrassing to him, and so, using the excuse that E.L. was looking a little cross-eyed, we thought we'd better adjourn.

We paid our bill and when we got to the border E.L. said, "American!" just in case they couldn't tell from his uniform.

We didn't have a trio get together again for a while after that. In fact E.L. asked to be reassigned as a pilot, which he qualified for and the reassignment was granted. It was a good move, and he was a lot happier person after that. But it did mean that we had to find a new co-pilot, which ended up taking some time.

E.L. wasn't the only crew member we had to replace. Our gunner with the sensitive stomach, Kirk, had previously applied for pilot training and they were now transferring him accordingly so that solved that problem, as the replacement could hold his stomach a little better. The next replacement to our crew was less positive, however. One morning in January Charlie woke me up early to tell me that Del had just been operated on for appendicitis. I was very surprised, as the previous night Del had complained of a slight stomach ache but had seemed ok otherwise. Charlie had found him out of sorts around midnight and had taken him to the aid station, and then to the hospital, where they decided to operate. It was a really unfortunate situation. Del was well-liked among the crew and was a skilled bombardier, but it looked like we would have to find someone else.

Charlie, E.L. and I visited Del when we could, but soon we met our new bombardier – Second Lieutenant Juvie Ortez. He seemed like a pretty nice fellow to me.

Although he had been a bombardier for over a year, mostly on anti-sub patrol in the Caribbean area, he hadn't really had a lot of bombing practice with a Norden bombsight, a special sight that was secret at the time. But he did have a pretty neat car, a '42 Chevrolet. Juvie soon got acquainted with the group, but we still remained in contact with Del in and out of his hospital time.

And so our training continued. We were still in our second phase of combat training, but were on course to be stationed in England. A lot of our training involved formation flying and cross-country missions, though there were also many hours spent on the ground. I didn't find ground school to be the most interesting subject, though there were exceptions. During one lesson a captain from the anti-aircraft outfit at Fort Bliss told us quite a bit about how the anti-aircraft outfits operate. He really impressed us with the potency of such an attack. First Lieutenant Benson, a bombardier from the 457th, tried to tell us how to survive anti-aircraft, but it seemed to be mainly a matter of luck. I was surprised to learn that Benson was a member of one of the fortresses (B-17s) that flew over to England along with my brother Bill. I spoke with him later and he said he thought he knew Bill.

January 23rd, 1944

Third phase officially started today – the time is slipping by. Bill is missing for one year today.

Starting our third phase of combat training meant more specified courses, and more waking up early in the morning. Oh how I hated getting up in the morning! Practicing at the gunnery range was one of these new courses. At one of our first sessions we arrived at about 07:30 and spent the whole morning there. I fired about 150 rounds of .50 caliber machine gun ammunition. It wasn't so bad, but a lot of time was spent loafing around. I did see two coyotes on the way out there though. Later in the day, at 13:00, we reported for flying. The missions were often exhausting. On this particular day Charlie was grounded on account of his ears, the altitude caused a lot of sinus problems, so he didn't fly with us. We also still didn't have a co-pilot since E.L. had left, so we borrowed a co-pilot from another crew and got about three and a half hours of formation time. Practically all of it was at 20,000 feet and it got pretty cold, about minus twenty degrees Celsius (-4°F). The formation wasn't so bad, but I didn't get into position right like I should have at the beginning. I also didn't get my boots on right away and one foot got frozen up a bit, but I was sure glad I had one of the new (A-14) oxygen masks. All of us felt pretty tired when we got down.

The mornings were usually filled with ground school and the afternoons with flying. Ground school contained a lot of U.K. (United Kingdom) procedures, though sometimes I felt like I wasn't learning much. Flying was always interesting, as there were often last minute changes due to things such as the weather, and you had to stay on your toes. In one instance we were scheduled to drop twenty bombs at high altitude. At the last minute we were told to take off in a different position of the eighteen-ship formation than originally planned. We barely got our engines run up in time to take off to adjust. After we landed, a first lieutenant said I had been much too slow in getting into formation, but as far as I was concerned it was a matter of opinion. Our new bombardier Juvie dropped fifteen bombs and did pretty fair work – the first few were a little wild but some were very good. He did okay though considering everything.

More high altitude training was scheduled the next day since the weather had botched our plans the day before. This time we were number three in the first element, and so we had to fly on the left wing of the lead ship, something I had been weak on. Generally the formation went along fine except that I didn't intercept the first ship very well after takeoff. This meant I overran it considerably and then had to wait for him to catch me. On the record, the mission wasn't very successful, also because we lost two generators while climbing with altitude, but I did gain confidence in flying on the left wing.

January 30ᵗʰ, 1944

Had an ear ache after landing – the doctor put me on DNIF (duty not including flying) so I guess I won't fly tomorrow as scheduled (have to be on the line early anyway though).

February 1st, 1944

Another B-24 from the field crashed and burned – all men (seven) parachuted to safety.

Crashes and accidents continued to happen around us during training, but I tried to stay focused. Our next training mission was a long cross-country to Fort Worth and return. The weatherman said we would have to fly around 15,000 feet or so in order to get over the lower layers of cumulus clouds, which were dangerous to come across in the sky. It was late when we started, but we took off an hour later than planned at 21:30. At around 9,000 feet we hit the overcast and kept climbing through the clouds up to for 14,000 feet. These were the most genuine instruments conditions I had ever flown in. At around 23,000 feet we finally broke out of it by Big Springs and flew on to Fort Worth. By the time we made it back it was past three in the morning, and my jaw was really aching from biting down on the constant-flow oxygen mask. I didn't get to bed until after five and slept until 11:00 the next morning, but the instrument practice was very worthwhile.

February 5th, 1944

Learned that one B-24 from our squadron crashed and burned on the McNavy bomb range last night and all six men were killed. Don't know much about it. It is odd that they couldn't have jumped as they are not supposed to be flying lower on the bomb range.

Had the whole day off. Intended to go to the show in the evening but fell asleep. Charlie was with Virginia and E.L., and Juvie had dates with a couple of nurses. I wish Del was still here.

Last night Major Fletcher announced that quite a few crews were going to leave in a week. We weren't on the list but it is subject to change. I am not so eager anyway, as they will have to fly every day now and nothing has been said to indicate they are getting a good deal.

After weeks of waiting we were finally introduced to our new co-pilot, Second Lieutenant Roy Walser. He was at the line with us for the first time when we were set for a

U.K. navigation-trainer mission. Roy seemed to be okay.

On our first gunnery training session together as a crew we arrived just in time to see the trucks pull out for the range. We waited around for a few minutes and then tore back to the sack. Perhaps not the best exercise as a crew, but that was our decision. That afternoon we were watching the eighteen-ship formation flying overhead when a couple of ships suddenly dove out of formation and four parachutes blossomed out of one. That B-24 made a wide circle of the field at a rather low altitude and then came in and managed to land okay. Later we learned the details: Lieutenant Lloyd's left wing touched Gurman while in formation. This caused Gurman and the instructor pilot to lose control for a few seconds, and the plane started to lose altitude in a dive. In doing so it struck another ship from the formation below. Gurman then ordered all able men out, but couldn't leave himself because a couple of his men in the rear of the ship were knocked out. They were losing 150 feet a minute, but had managed to land. All three ships involved landed okay and no one was seriously hurt. Lieutenant Lloyd's left wing was pretty well banged up and Gurman's right rudder was useless. In addition, he had a large hole underneath his fuselage. Nevertheless, things could have been much worse.

Flying with Roy was an adjustment at first. I didn't have the confidence in him that I had in E.L., and although he did pretty good sometimes, while landing he came in too close once or twice. Our crew was slowly coming together, and during some rare down time I was able to have a good talk with the enlisted men. We had a very good enlisted crew, including Sergeant Hanwell, our radio operator. However, there was the possibility that changes would come again to the crew and that Hanwell would be washed back because he was behind due to time in the hospital. It was eventually decided that he would be kept on the crew. He was a good boy, and eager, and I was glad that he stayed.

February 9th, 1944

Up for a malaria lecture at the theatre. Afterwards had a very interesting lecture by a British squadron leader who was a gunnery expert. He had been on two combat tours with the R.A.F (600 hours) and 593 hours with the U.S. Air Force in the Middle East, etc. He really seemed to know his business and said the B-24 was a real ship. In reply to B-17 men he said, "Why take a hand grenade up to 30,000 feet?"

Another new specified course in the third level of combat training was chemical warfare. In our first session there was an interesting lecture, a movie, and a few demonstrations of smoke bombs and incendiaries. Then the pilots went down to the pistol range to fire the .45. I enjoyed it quite a bit. Later that day, though, we had a night bombing and navigation mission, and it just turned out to be a horrible mess. Charlie set the course, but winds blew us away from the area. We were supposed to drop ten bombs at Alamogordo at high altitude, and then go to Midland and Pyrte on a cross-country. As we were going to Alamogordo, I started trying to get the auto-pilot set up and apparently wandered all over the country. When it was finally set up at 20,000 feet, Juvie saw a bomb range and although the targets and some surroundings looked odd, we assumed it was Alamogordo just the same. After we dropped the bombs and started back to the airbase, we decided it hadn't been Alamogordo. After flying around a while we finally concluded it was Roswell, but by then we had to return to Biggs as it was getting late. When we returned to the field the number three engine pump was out and wouldn't lower the landing gear, a problem indeed. However, the auxiliary hydraulic pump and star valve did the trick and we called it a day. We never mentioned what we had done. It could have caused a bad accident. So we just kept that under the rug, so to speak.

February 18th, 1944

Didn't get to bed until 05:00 this morning, so even if we did sleep until almost 12:00, we didn't get an over amount of rest. At 12:00 we had a dental inspection for the crew and then had ground school.

Down to the line at 18:30. We were scheduled to drop ten bombs at high altitude and then go on a cross-country, but we never got off of the ground. The generator panel shorted out just before takeoff. We had to wait around until around 13:00 and then went home.

A surprising, yet encouraging, bit of news came when I was sent over to the Sergeant Major's office at base headquarters. There I learned I had been recommended for First Lieutenant. I considered myself quite lucky, as it is good to have it before going overseas. Also the sergeant said that they hadn't promoted any combat crew officers at this post for the past eight months.

Our main instructor, Major Fletcher, held a critique after each practice mission for the pilots. I really enjoyed these and after he got through expressing his thoughts, he was open for questions. I frequently would hold up my hand to say what I had in mind. I did it so often that I was expecting to hear groans from the other pilots whenever I raised my hand, but they never came. The major seemed to think they were good, valid questions and would give more details. This impressed him, and he decided I was a 'good boy', and I ended up getting a superior rating from him. I admired the major for the job he was doing. His face was badly scarred due to a crash landing he made while in Australia flying a B-24 earlier in the war against Japan. He was a good leader. He could chew you out or praise you, depending on what you deserved.

Upon my return I learned that Charlie had been having more trouble with his ears and, for good reasons, he thought he might be grounded for good. However, he took a test later and managed to get by okay. I sure would have hated to lose him.

February 21st, 1944

Had a dental appointment at 08:30 and had three teeth filled. Once they get going on you, these army dentists don't stop for nothing until they finish. It doesn't take long that way.

Couldn't get our orders today but learned that we were on the McCook list alright.

We were issued a ten day leave so we could go home, and then we were to report to McCook, Nebraska to join the 493rd bomb group to get additional training. We were to learn that this would be the last group to join the 8th Air Force in England. Others who were not so lucky would be sent as individual replacement crews to the 8th. Our bomb group, the 493rd, had four squadrons, the 860th, 861st, 862nd, and 863rd. My squadron was the 862nd, which included crews of B-17 and B-24 bombers, and we were led by Major Pete Sianis as squadron commander.

I left the day after for good ol' Missoula for my leave, though it took a while to get there. I got away rather late in the afternoon and drove to Albuquerque, enjoying the ride with Juvie in his car. I wasn't able to take the train to Denver, but caught a train to La Junta because it was four hours late. I slept most of the night sitting up on the train. From then on I made my own travel arrangements and arrived in Missoula on February 26th. It was great to be home again and to be with the folks and Shep, of course, but the time went by quickly while visiting with friends and family. As usual, at the end of my leave the folks drove with me to Butte and I enjoyed the beautiful scenery along the way. Then I left by train for McCook. It was a sad day saying goodbye.

Part 4:

Overseas

The crew: McCook Army Air Base – April 6, 1944
Front row (left to right): Sgt. Carl Halteman (gunner), Sgt. Sam Owens (gunner), Sgt.
James Hanwell (radio operator), Sgt. Marion Rutherford (gunner), Sgt. Leo Mason
(gunner)
Back row (left to right): 2nd Lt. Charles Gray (navigator), 2nd Lt. Roy Walser (co-pilot), 1st
Lt. Robert Schottelkorb (pilot), 2nd Lt. Juvie Ortiz (bombardier), S/Sgt. Victor Andersen
(engineer)

I arrived in McCook on March 5th, 1944 at about eight in the evening and met Roy. We got a cold ride to the base in a G.I. truck, signed in, and went to our barracks. Our other crew members, Juvie and Charlie, were also already there. For the months of March and April we started more intense training for when we would be sent overseas. Much of the training was flying formation, something I found to be pretty tricky, and I was sure glad Roy could fly formation ok as it made it a lot easier for me. When we weren't flying we were in ground school, and I still often felt like I wasn't learning anything new. Sometimes I goofed off during the lessons, mostly because I was disgusted with the same old stuff all the time.

In my down time I wrote letters home, read, and got sleep when I could. In the evenings the crew officers and I went to shows and on dates. I went on quite a few dates with a girl named Donna. She was a nice girl, didn't drink or smoke, and we got along fine, but we never did get very serious about a future together. We went to many dances along with Charlie and his date, and I thought it was good to celebrate before we left for combat.

Pretty soon, however, our turn to head overseas as part of the 8th Air Force came and we flew to Lincoln, Nebraska for processing. We were issued some really good flying equipment and also the inspectors went through all of our belongings including my neatly packed footlocker. They wouldn't let us take some things overseas, so I ended up sending a lot of junk home. The base in Lincoln wasn't a bad base in some respects - efficient, green grass all around, etc, but our particular barracks wasn't so hot, it was like an empty barn with beds in it. No nails or benches to hang clothes on. No facilities for writing. Also the town and base were pretty crowded.

Our crew was issued a shiny new B-24J, J indicating the new model designation. They had recently discontinued spraying the planes with camouflage paint because it didn't achieve any advantage. It handled well and seemed to have quite a bit of speed. I didn't have time to check everything though, and once after landing a calibration mission Charlie plotted his readings and found that it was way off, so bad in fact that we weren't able to

Hanwell and Mason in the new B-24

leave when scheduled and were delayed a day.

Around one in the morning on May 12th we were awakened and soon afterwards were taken over to the mess hall via G.I. truck to get our last meal at Lincoln. After breakfast we had a briefing on our trip and the weather, route, etc. The local weather wasn't very good but they were anxious to have us on our way, so we left around 03:00 in a rain shower with lightning flashing in the vicinity. It was fairly rough and turbulent for a while but at 3,000 feet we were able to fly contact most of the way to Moliere, Iowa (via Omaha and Des Moines). From Moliere on it wasn't bad at all and, of course, it began to get light as the sun came up. We flew the airways most of the way. After Moliere came Joliet, Goshen, Toledo, Cleveland, Erie, Buffalo, and Rochester.

At Buffalo I decided to take a side trip to view Niagara Falls. I don't remember asking Charlie, I simply said, "Let's go take a look at Niagara Falls!"

It was off-limits to fly directly over so we just stayed off to the side and didn't linger, but we just got a view of it and years later the wife of the crew chief that flew with us mentioned that as he saw out of the waist windows of the plane he thought just how beautiful it was. At Rochester we were ordered to change course and fly to Grenier Field in Manchester, New Hampshire. After a long flight of nearly eight and a half hours we landed at 12:30. We were rather tired but the auto pilot had done most of the work.

May 13th, 1944

Today was apparently our last day in the good old USA for some time as this field is to be our port of embarkation from USA to Canada. We arrived here at Grenier Field only yesterday noon, but they don't believe in wasting any time, and so after a rather short night of rest we are ready to move on.

At 08:00 we were briefed again on our trip to Goose Bay, Labrador. I filled out a clearance and gathered up the required manuals while Charlie made out our flight plan.

Takeoff was at 10:00 and so at long last it seemed as if we were going to actually go overseas. We flew the radio range to Portland, August, Millinocket, and Presque Isle, Maine. The latter was the last point in the U.S. and from there on we flew according to Charlie's D.R. (dead reckoning) calculations. We crossed over the little port of Campbellton on course and then headed over the Bay of St. Lawrence to Mingan. All of this time we were on the auto-pilot and it was doing a good job of holding our course and so Roy and I were able to take it comparatively easy. We got off course to the right while over the bay as we had nothing to go by except the forecast winds; however, we were able to correct to the left before long as we had a good pilotage point to go by – (the tip of an island in the bay). Not long after that we picked up the Mingan beam and followed it on in. While over the bay, Roy saw a sperm whale spouting, but otherwise there wasn't much to report.

I got out my camera and we started taking pictures of the crew up front. We had it on automatic pilot and hopefully some of us were watching for other possibility of aircraft in the vicinity, but we did have kind of a little celebration there in the cockpit area and took pictures of several of us. That camera was pretty nice to bring out at times.

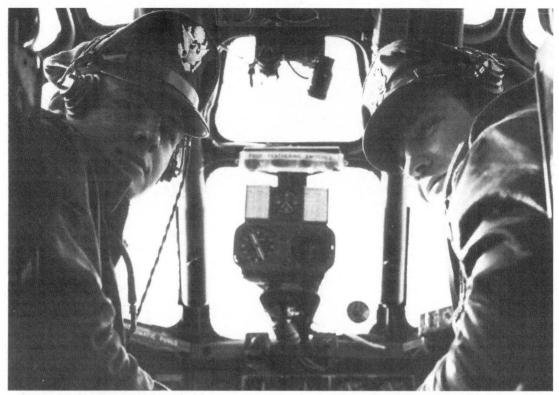

Up front with Roy Walser

Hanwell, our
radio operator
and youngest
crew member at
age 19

After passing over Mingan the country became quite rugged and desolate. It wouldn't be very good country to be forced down in – especially in winter. We arrived at Goose Bay in the early afternoon after an easy trip. We also enjoyed unusually good weather for this part of the country as it is often necessary to make an instrument let down through the often present low clouds and fog. The field here is very good – the runways are 6000 feet long, 200 feet wide and flat as a table. When we parked the ship we turned on the oil dilution switches for about a minute so that the oil wouldn't be too thick when we had to start the engines again. It was rather cool alright even in the afternoon sun. Before long we had signed in and had been assigned to our respective barracks.

May 15th, 1944

Ordinarily we would have taken off yesterday, the 14th, but the weather prevented this. It was snowing when we woke up, but we were just as glad, as we got to get a good rest and sleep in late for a change.

Today the weather was better so we were to report for briefing at 18:30. The pilots were briefed mostly on the route, emergency procedures, and weather. I couldn't help but feel excited about it. At first it seemed like a lot of water to be flying over. We took off in the evening so that we could use celestial navigation and land in Iceland in daylight. We took off at 22:25 and at 22:32 we were over the field and heading on course to Iceland. It was still light as we left the coast.

The sun was very reluctant to descend so we followed Charlie's flight plan for several hours. We were able to get a check on our ground speed by our time, made good to the south beam of the Port Christian (Greenland) radio range. It didn't get dark until after 1 am and at that time Charlie was able to get a three star fix, which showed us to be on course. Shortly after that it was too light for him to make any more shots, so from then on we flew according to the flight plan (and forecast metro information) until we reached the Meeks Field radio range. Most of the way we flew at 11,000 feet but also flew at 15,000 feet for a couple hours as per flight plan. The weather forecast was quite accurate except that we ran into some clouds above 15,000 feet for a while. I watched for icing, but apparently the conditions weren't just right (it was pretty cold) or else the heat in the wings (when I turned on the wing heating unit[1]) prevented it. At any rate everything went pretty smoothly and I was certainly thankful that we had such a good auto pilot. When we got closer to Iceland we picked up the beam and followed it in. We all made bets on Charlie's ETA (estimated time of arrival). He ended up being overdue about 40 minutes and he lost a $5.00 bet to Roy and a $1.00 bet to me.

---

[1] Located on the edge of the wing where ice would form, it seemed to work pretty well. It was nice to have that feature in the later models.

Landing at Meeks in Iceland around 06:00 it was plenty light and we could see that it was a rather bare and desolate looking place. The long hours of light and the mixed up schedule certainly made us lose all track of time. The crude living conditions (poor plumbing, etc.) of this field sure makes us realize how lucky we've been in the States. The enlisted men around here say that they aren't treated very well in town and so they mostly just stay on base.

We went to the show at 21:00 but were routed out half way through the picture by an air raid alarm. The way everyone took out of there and got their rifles ready, etc. sure looked like the real thing – especially to us who had never had any contact with any raids of war. Apparently a few enemy planes were supposed to be in the vicinity but nothing happened and before long it was called off.

We got to bed around midnight but we didn't get much sleep as they unexpectedly decided to have briefing a lot earlier than anticipated, so we were awakened at 03:00. After a rather skimpy breakfast of one fried egg and oatmeal with powdered milk we took a G.I. truck to briefing and from there to our airplane.

At 05:00 we were on our way to Prestwick, Scotland. Our route took us over the north Atlantic to the airport at Stornoway located off the northern tip of Scotland on a rocky island. Our ETA for Stornoway was off about 30 minutes and we wound up considerably south of course due to the poor metro winds we had been given. Also the radio range was apparently being meaconed[2] as the radio compass was off considerably. (We later learned that others had had the same trouble) As we approached the coast the ceiling lowered and we got down pretty low over the water trying to get under the ceiling. After we had done this we found we were too low to cross over the cliff of the Scottish coast so we climbed up over the layer of clouds again. Roy wanted to try to go in under the clouds but it looked impossible.

I didn't want to take a chance flying low under the clouds. Roy was different than me though and I knew he wanted to be a fighter pilot. Those planes could maneuver and move around easily, but that was not the case with the B-24.

After we were above clouds we weren't very sure of our position so we resorted to a QDM[3]. We couldn't get it over the command set and Hanwell couldn't get contact with the

---

[2] Jammed by the Germans
[3] Request for a compass heading

liaison set but the VHF[4] set did the trick. They gave us the heading to follow and we came right in over the field. They told us to go on to Prestwick (Scotland) as we were originally scheduled. We had been scheduled to fly this leg of the trip contact but we had an undercast for a while and couldn't. Later on the undercast broke up and we were able to use pilotage points along the Scottish coast. At Prestwick we had to fly over the top, so we had to make an instrument letdown on the range there. We broke out at 3,000 feet and made it ok, although the visibility was pretty poor. We landed after a tiring 6:45 hours and were met at the plane by a captain who informed us we have to fly on to our home field in short order. After a few donuts and hot coffee and a short briefing, eight of us B-24s took off for our new base – Debach. We followed the lead plane flown by a Lieutenant who really knew the country, to us it looked all the same. We flew all the way at low altitude in a fairly loose formation. We arrived at Debach in early evening and were met by a truck and loaded everything from the plane onto it. A few crews were already here – in fact Lt. Shipley cracked up[5] on landing. Guess he overshot and was too proud to go around. I guess he really is a good pilot.

Again, I had followed in Bill's footsteps. Bill had left for England July 25th, 1942 from Goose Bay, Labrador and arrived in England by way of Greenland, Iceland, and Scotland. Their journey, however, had been much more difficult. They had encountered many weather delays, especially in Iceland. I can't imagine how difficult it had been for him to fly with his small squadron over to England. When I flew over I had a navigator, co-pilot, engineer, radio-operator, and all the help I needed. Bill had been alone in his cramped cockpit and relied on visual contact with the B-17 while facing all kinds of weather. At times the visibility got down to eight feet. In fact the army discontinued trying to escort P-38s over the ocean because the 1st Fighter Group had to crash land in Greenland just about ten days before Bill flew over. That was called 'the lost squadron' although they all survived. Years later at least one P-38 was brought up through about 200 feet of ice and snow that had accumulated on it and it is now an iconic reminder of that flight. Bill was really lucky to complete the flight with his difficulties. To top it off, Bill ran into electrical problems when he was near Iceland. He lost his automatic adjustment for his prop switch and he had to use manual control instead. This especially makes it

---

[4] Very High-Frequency radio
[5] Crashed

difficult when trying to land, as he had many other things to worry about during such a procedure. I was proud that I completed the flight, but boy I can't imagine flying in the conditions Bill experienced.

Bill with his P-38

From the day of our arrival in Debach, May 17th, until D-day, June 6th, we had no operational flights. These days were spent going to ground school and on practice formation flights.

During this time our crew got mixed around a bit. They wanted to take Charlie away from us and he wanted to stay with us. The commanders compromised; sometimes they'd take him and we'd have to get somebody else, but most the time he was able to stay with us, and that made me very happy.

When June 6th came around we weren't called up. Some were disappointed and felt a little guilty, but I didn't figure I had to be in any particular battle or mission.

June 6th, 1944 –D-Day

Today the long awaited invasion started. It was an important day for two reasons:

(1) The invasion started

(2) The 493rd Group became operational (finally)! The latter is a sure indication that we are in an all-out effort.

The mission was led by the good Lt. Col. himself and he did a pretty good job even though he couldn't drop the bombs. Some flak[6] was encountered and he detoured around it nicely. This first mission cost our own squadron two crews – the first casualties so far – and on our first mission for the group.

Capt. Cooper and First Lt. Russell were the two pilots involved. Cooper was flying the number seven position (leading the third element) and Russell was flying number ten (leading the fourth element). Cooper dropped down at the same time Russell overshot and slid underneath him and the two ships collided and broke apart. Wager saw it all happen and I guess it was quite a sight. Collisions of these planes especially are bad business. Cooper especially seemed to be a good pilot. It is believed one or two men out of the twenty may have bailed out ok.

June 7th, 1944

Today was to be our first mission but it turned out to be kind of a mess. They tried to get us up into the blue without any notice but it didn't work. None of the crews or guns or airplanes were ready at takeoff time and so they didn't get together decently for assembly. Some were still taking off when we were supposed to be well on our way towards our target – a railroad bridge near Tours, France. We got together with our own leader, but there were only five of us when we were about halfway across the channel and we were ordered to return to base. It was a rather black mark against the 493rd and later we had a meeting with the Colonel and tried to organize a better setup and correct our mistakes. We hope we don't have another deal like that. We also learned that a few of the boys tacked on to other groups and went on to the target. (Mims, Hansen and Digges). Lt. Digges of the 863rd squadron is missing in action. He was hit by flak over the target with another group.

June 12th, 1944 – MISSION #1 – 6:00 hours

Today we had our first mission. We were awakened before 1 am this morning and after a quick breakfast we had briefing at 01:45. Our target was an airfield north of Paris, nearly two miles north of the town of Beauvais. Takeoff was at 05:00 and before long we were assembling at 17,000 feet over splasher number six[7]. We had to climb through a slight overcast for a while due to weather. B-24s and B-17s were all over the sky and it was quite a sight.

We were one of the spares and Capt. Whitlock was too, so Charlie flew with us instead. Everything went along ok until we reached the French coast and then the lead ship, Maj. Hale, tried to abort, but the deputy lead, Maj. Orban, screwed up and tried to follow him. The whole squadron broke up like a covey of quail. We didn't know whether to join another group and go on to target, or to stick it out with our own outfit. I decided we should do the latter and about that time our leader struck off like a scalded goose and tried to catch up with the group ahead without trying to get our outfit together. Several of us had already aborted and the rest were strung out all over the place. We could just see what a target we would be for enemy fighters, but I determined to catch up if at all possible. I can still remember Charlie saying, "Bob, you are perfectly justified to turn around and go back". I have to admit it was rather uncomfortable to be back there, but we weren't the only ones. We had a heavy load of frags[8] and were pulling just about full power – 2650 rpm & 47 inch[9] manifold pressure. When we finally caught up everyone flew more or less in a bunch and no one held their position. It was rather a mess. To top it off Juvie tied up and dropped his bombs too early by mistake. It sure made him feel bad, too. The rest of the group did do some fair bombing I guess. Fortunately we encountered no fighters and only a puff or two of flak. We suffered no losses. I was really pooped afterwards and got only a couple of hours of sleep before being awakened for another meeting by the Colonel.

That's one thing about a bomber; you just keep plugging along and take it as long as the leader is showing you the way. I also never wanted to turn back from a mission unless I was ordered to. If you didn't complete your mission you wouldn't get credit for it, and we had to complete 30 missions in order to go back home.

During our missions I had the notion that I was the pilot. I was supposed to get our

---

[6] Exploding artillery from ground based heavy guns
[7] Ground based radio beacon
[8] Smaller bombs that explode into deadly fragments, against personnel
[9] Measurement of the power applied by the engine throttle: the higher the number, the greater the power

plane to the target and get the bombs dropped, and then I would turn the controls over to Roy. Of course, there were periods while we were flying it was good to have him relieve me on route to the target, for instance during our ascent. Once we'd taken off and slowly climbed with the heavy bomb load and load of fuel, we'd gain altitude by flying in large circles spread over quite an area. It was a routine. We would go so many minutes climbing and circling until the radio signal, the buncher, would point us in the right direction. While we were making this slow climb, sometimes sleep would overcome me, since our missions were often at early morning hours, and I would let Roy take over. I would nod my head and take a little nap about five or ten minutes long, just as I'd done as a paper boy. Déjà vu!

Roy was quite competent and I had confidence in him so I never talked about it or broadcasted it, but he was flying the airplane at that time until I suddenly woke up and took over again. He didn't tell me this at first, but he said on the way to the target he was freezing, since there was basically very little physical movement. He never complained until he mentioned it later on in our tour. While I was steamed up and perspiring from the activity and stress of flying in formation, it was just the opposite for him. Roy said that once I turned the controls over to him after the bombs were away, so that he could make the return flight, he warmed up.

We also had heavy flak vests and steel helmets we could put on if we expected flak ahead. It was awkward, but when you see all that flak coming you think maybe I better get it on. When we got close to a target on the last set for the bombing run I would have my goggles on too and they wanted to steam up since I was running hot, so I thought maybe if I had to bail out it wouldn't be good to have the goggles, the moisture could have frozen and I wouldn't have seen a thing until I threw off the goggles. I am thankful I didn't have to test that theory.

June 15th, 1944 – MISSION #2 – 6:40 hours

Second mission and while it was better executed, it was also the roughest as far as we were concerned because of flak. This was another of those tiring all-night deals. We took off early in the morning and landed around 10:00. We led the low section in the lead squadron. Our target was an airfield just outside of Paris and our bombing altitude was 22,000 feet. Our ship that day, 170, an H[10], was a good ship but it sure was cold up there without those heaters. Everything went along good until we reached the target area. Our squadron bombardier couldn't find the target so he led us into the flak area. We bombed another target with not too good of results. We got pretty well sprayed. Hanwell said he had been hit and that caused quite a bit of confusion. While he had been hit, it was only that a piece of flak had hit a corner of his flying boot but had not hit him actually.

We were glad to be back on the ground as our gas was getting low. We spent quite a while looking over our ship. We counted about fifteen flak holes. They hit all over the place and it was a wonder that one of us didn't get hit. The hit that got Hanwell was a pretty big hole and it went through both sides of the waist and ripped through the reinforced flooring. Charlie was up on the flight deck navigating from the radio operators table and a piece of flak passed right under him and embedded itself in the bench across from him. Also had a

Looking over the flak damage with Andersen

[10] Aircraft number: H was the model letter of the B-24

hit on the back of the pilot's, and co-pilot's, seat. Other hits were found in a prop, a cowl flap, in the rudder, trailing edge of the wing, in an oxygen bottle in the waist and in the nose and tail turret. As long as it doesn't cause any more damage than that, typically flak is very sharp and jagged and makes nasty wounds, I guess it's ok.

Later we learned our right wing man had received a hit in the nose turret that had hit his nose gunner just below his flak helmet and had fractured his skull. Laderman was the pilot.

June 17th, 1944 – MISSION #3 – 6:50 hours

Had briefing at 00:30 this morning. Our target was an airfield near Angers, France. We taxied out and were just ready to take off when mission was scrubbed.

At 12:00 we had another briefing and this time we did get off ok. Our target was an airfield near Laval, France. We led the high element of the high squadron and in that position I had a good workout and had to do practically all the flying. On our way over the invasion coast we were able to see a battleship (probably the Texas) shelling the mainland. Shortly after this we saw a lone B-24 tagging along behind another group which was hit by a box barrage of flak over Caen. It really had its number and it burst into flames and blew apart. No chutes were seen. This little incident didn't help our morale any.

June 18th, 1944

Got to bed early in the morning and slept until 11:00 when we were put on standby. About 15:00 Capt. Hector came in and said we were on pass - 48 hours! It was a rather pleasant surprise and we left the base at 17:00 for Ipswich.

Took the train for London. We had a compartment to ourselves (four of us) and it was pretty nice. Arrived at Liverpool Station at 21:45 and tried to get a hotel. This proved to be quite a job as it was Sunday and late at that. We took a bus to get to the Strand Palace hotel but no rooms were available or at any other nearby hotels. Finally got a taxi after standing around for some time and went to the Hamilton House in Grosvenor Square and it proved to be somewhat of a dump, but was the best we could do at the time. Had several raids by the pilotless planes, which seem to have many of the Londoners rather jumpy.

June 19th, 1944

About 09:00 Juvie and Roy got Charlie and me up and we went down to breakfast at our hotel (on the European Plan). It sure was a skimpy breakfast. I wouldn't want that kind very often. We spent all morning shopping and generally looking the business district over.

We couldn't seem to find 8th Air Force patches to suit us. Had a drink or two and then went to eat dinner at a Russian restaurant which served pretty good food. During lunch an aerial bomb went off about half a mile away and so after we finished we went to see the damage. It hit a police station and wrecked buildings nearby. Also shattered all windows for about three blocks around it. About 65 people were believed to have been killed. Kind of hard on nerves of the Londoners.

June 22nd, 1944 – MISSION #4 – 6:40 hours

Had briefing at 12:30. It was rather short as we didn't have much time to spare. Then at the last minute we had everything cut short 45 minutes and we were unable to take off on time. I was attempting to lead the low section, but was having a hard time to keep up with the old clunker we were flying. It was 518, an H, that had been pawed off on our group in trade for one of our new Js. Before we had left England we discovered a leak in the bombardier's, nose gunner's, and navigator's oxygen systems. Just as we crossed the French coast we lost our number one turbo and could only draw 32 inches[11] on it. It wouldn't have been so bad with a good ship, but with this old tub it really made it bad. We were practically pulling full power all of the time, but we couldn't hold our position so we had our wing men go on and we tagged along behind as best we could.

When we finally got over the target area we circled around several times and flak was bursting all around us. We were to bomb rolling stock in the railroad center, but apparently they couldn't find anything to bomb so we dropped our bombs on an airfield. It was certainly a good thing that the leader dropped his bombs then (40-100 pound) because if he hadn't we would have dropped our own there because we thought we were about out of gas. Charlie had checked the gas gauges and we thought he said that we only had 50 gallons left in each tank which wouldn't last any time. Actually he had said 150 but everyone misunderstood him. It turned out ok, because we started heading back then, but we were sweating out the gas (and the ship). By this time our number three tachometer was out (as well as number four and three cylinder head temperature gauges). Just before our bombs were dropped our turbos began to oscillate wildly when high power settings were used. Number one was throwing quite a bit of oil too.

On the way back we dropped behind trying to conserve fuel and hold a steady power setting. Near the coast we got several bursts of flak to our right and we could tell they were after our own little plane. We turned off to the left and started our evasive action. Sure enough we looked over to where we would have been and there were about four bursts of flak in a row that would have had us. We continued to use evasive action and before long we were out of that area. Roy got quite a kick out of having the Germans waste their shells on us, but I would just as soon have them save them. About the time we got to

---

[11] Measurement of the power applied by the engine throttle: the higher the number, the greater the power

the coast we found we had more gas than we had thought and we were able to join the formation on the descent.

We landed at 9:30 pm about out of gas. By this time we also had a few more things wrong with the ship and we really had a full page of write ups for the ship. Had a hard time getting the flaps down and then they wouldn't come up. The auxiliary power unit wouldn't start either[12].

It was rather a hectic day for us although we were fortunate in not getting any flak hits. Enemy fighters were supposed to have been shot down in the target area, but we didn't encounter any (fortunate for us).

Wager about cracked up when coming in for a landing as all four engines quit at once. They were out of gas but his engineer managed to transfer a little fuel from the auxiliaries just in the nick of time.

Lt. Kaplan of our squadron is missing in action. It is believed that he was hit by flak just east of Le Havre on his return home. He had been forced to drop out of formation as we had, and was by himself when it happened. So not too much is known about what did happen.

Couldn't seem to get a good rest as I have kept dreaming about running out of fuel, getting flak, and fighting prop wash[13]. Send me back to Missoula!

June 23rd, 1944 – MISSION #5 – 6:45 hours

Briefed at 13:00 today to bomb an airfield a little northeast of Paris. Major Whitlock led the group and we were in the second squadron with Lt. Conger and Capt. Simmons leading it. We led the high element again. I would just as soon not fly in the high element at all. I dropped back at times and, all in all, I guess I gave my wing men plenty of trouble, but we all had our troubles.

We didn't encounter any flak over the target area, but weren't able to drop our bombs due to the undercast. We tried to find a target of opportunity for a while, but after a bit of circling we headed back and didn't drop our bombs. Our route back took us over Belgium and Holland over a solid undercast. We got a little off course and our squadron picked up some flak. Our plane got three holes in it. One piece was embedded in our emergency radio and Rutherford dug it out as a souvenir.

---

[12] That plane should have been scrapped!
[13] Rough air/turbulence created by other aircraft at the same altitude

This was another fairly easy mission although we didn't like to bring our bombs back. We were pretty well played out[14] when we landed, as it was our second mission in the last two days.

June 24th, 1944

Enjoyed a good night's sleep, as I was pretty tired after two missions in two days. Took a shower, shave and went to dinner.

I spent the afternoon washing a few clothes and generally puttering around. Also enjoyed about an hour in the sun - quite a luxury in the ETO[15]. Apparently our group only had one mission today and that started shortly after we landed last night. They encountered plenty of flak. Lewis' co-pilot was hit in the hand by flak. Our 'hut mates' - Kolloff & crew went on pass today.

Kolloff was the pilot of another crew that shared living quarters with us. He was an easy-going guy, big and friendly. A good guy all around.

Got a lift in morale from three letters - one from Jay (a 1st Lt. now), Mother and Clark MacDonald.

June 25th, 1944 – MISSION #6 – 7:00 hours

Briefed at 1 am this morning. The target was another airfield in France: St. Avord. It is approximately six miles southeast of Bourges. Our group consisting of two squadrons along with one from the 34th led the entire division.

We took off at 04:00 and on our climb to assembly altitude over buncher 27[16] we thought we saw a J-88[17] pass high and to the front of us. Either it was not a Jerry or he didn't see us - at any rate he didn't bother us. We didn't have any trouble assembling except for some prop wash for a bit. We flew the number eleven position in the second squadron. It was the first time we had flown a wing position for a long time. We didn't try to hold in real tight. We had a pretty easy time of it.

Our bombing altitude was 20,000 feet and we had very good visibility. We plastered the

---

[14] Exhausted
[15] European Theater of Operations
[16] Radio beacon to hone in on while flying
[17] German light bomber plane

target with forty 100-pound bombs. The only opposition encountered was moderate flak along the route and it wasn't close to us. P-38s & P-51s[18] provided cover all of the way. One of our boys was having trouble with his number two engine and it was smoking badly. After the target Glotfelty dropped behind and when we got near the French coast on the return we lost track of him. No one knew what happened to him for a while, but a few days later he showed up ok. He had made an emergency landing on one of the fighter strips in France with P-38's escorting him down.

Another group's mission to Hanover, Germany left a few of the boys a little shaken up and nervous. All the boys agreed that the flak was rough and plenty had numerous holes to prove it. One of our boys in the next hut, Lt. Hansen, received a direct hit and went down in flame, literally. He apparently got several direct bursts of flak. No chutes were seen and at least most of the crew is believed to be lost. Old Mac, Lloyd's co-pilot, saw Hansen get knocked down off of their left wing and he became rather nervous. I can't say I blame him.

June 26th, 1944 – commissioned one year ago

June 30th, 1944 – MISSION #7 – 5:30 hours

This morning we briefed at 06:00 in spite of bad weather. Our target was again an airfield in France (two miles east of Evreux), but this time we were going to go ahead and drop bombs whether we had an overcast over the target or not. Each of our two squadrons was led by a special ship from another group, which was equipped with special G-box equipment for dropping bombs through an overcast by radar.

We had just started our engines when we were told to cut them and wait for an hour and a half. We finally took off at 10:30 and by then the weather was better. It was a little harder to assemble than usual as it was at 22,000 feet - our bombing altitude. After we did tack on to our leader everything went along pretty well. For one thing we were leading the low section again and it is about as good a position as you can get.

We dropped our bombs with the leader through the clouds so we don't know the results. Encountered only a puff or two of flak way off to our left once. P-51s provided us with

---

[18] American pursuit fighter planes: P-38 Lightning, P-51 Mustang

good cover. This flight was really a 'milk run'[19].

July 1st, 1944

Today I slept in until 10:30 and when I got up my boys had already left for London. After getting up I changed my linen on my bed and got my laundry and took it over to the laundry site on my bicycle. Then made an appointment for a haircut and went to eat. After dinner I started to go get my haircut and discovered someone had borrowed my bicycle and wrecked the rear wheel. I am pretty sure it is a certain person but cannot prove it so I guess I will have to let it go. It is too bad some fellows are so dishonest.

Got paid after getting the haircut and spent the rest of the afternoon doing a little washing and reading. Spent the evening batting the breeze with Kolloff and crew. No one flew today due to weather so they are having it easy too.

On July 4, 1944 all of us in our crew and another crew, Lieutenant Wollford's, were presented the air medal by Coronal Helton in a brief ceremony. The 8th Air Force gave awards for crew members who had completed seven missions. The air medal came complete with a nice blue cloth-covered case with a satin interior, as well as a statement of the achievement. Another cardboard box for shipping was included so it could be mailed home, and this is what I did without telling Mom and Dad. Later, Mom sent me a touching letter saying they were almost overwhelmed with emotion when they received it. It was pride mixed with the worry of me becoming a casualty.

July 8th, 1944 – MISSION #8 – 4:45 hours

Today two squadrons of our group had assignments to bomb a "no-ball target" (or a rocket gun installation near the French coast). This proved to be our shortest mission so far as we only logged four and three fourths hours.

We briefed at 01:15 and had plenty of time to spare before takeoff at 04:30. We had a pretty good ship, 418, a J, and never had to pull excessive power with it. We assembled as usual at buncher 27 at 15,000 feet. We climbed to bombing level on course and reached 23,000 feet by the time we had left England.

---

[19] An easy mission: coined with the idea of the delivery of milk in cities

Over France our two squadrons split up to bomb separate targets. We were leading the low element of the lead squadron. Although we were to be over France for less than an hour we were expecting flak and we got it alright. We didn't encounter any over the target at all but did on two or three occasions on the way to it. They really had us cased down well and they were bursting all around us. We could feel the impact of the explosions on the ship and I thought for sure that we would be riddled. After we landed we were surprised to find only three flak holes and none of them seemed to indicate that it had much power to it. Maybe these weren't as big of guns as those we have encountered previously. At any rate they should have done a lot more than they did. We prefer it this way.

We did a pretty fair job of bombing and our ship dropped its twenty 250-pound bombs along with the rest. The target was well camouflaged in a forest. We landed at 09:00. An easy mission except for the flak. As far as we know everyone returned safely.

July 11th, 1944

We slept in fairly late again - in fact I overslept. They say the CQ[20] woke me about 08:00 and told me we were to brief for a practice mission at 09:00, but I couldn't remember anything about it. Guess I was up to my old tricks and didn't even wake up enough to get the score. By the time I got up it was about 09:30 and too late to go on the mission. It was supposed to be another navigation mission. We are to have two such flights. Expected to fly in the afternoon but it was raining a lot and all they had was a combat mission which was scrubbed due to weather. Fortunately we weren't even on it.

Went to a show in the evening "Four Jills in a Jeep". Pretty fair. Another good rumor – the 3rd division, our division, is going to be converted to all B-17s (we are about half 17s and half 24s now) In other words we will start flying 17s. It would be a change but I don't know if I would care for a 17.

July 18th, 1944 – MISSION #9 – 5:10 hours

This morning our group put up 42 planes in a rather unusual type of bombing for heavy bombers. Our wing and many other heavies[21] of the second division were assigned an area to plaster with bombs in direct support of British troops who were to start a drive after the bombing ceased. The area was southwest of Cagny, not far from Caen.

We took off at 05:00 and assembled without incident as lead of the high element in 'C' squadron. Capt. Lloyd led us and everything was ok except for the darn prop wash from

---

[20] Charge of Quarters. An enlisted man from operations would report orders to us regardless of the time, day or night.

[21] Wing: a divisional term under which are three or four bomb groups; Heavies: four-engine bombers

the lead squadron. It really takes the joy out of flying (if there is any to start with). Several times it forced me out of formation.

We came in at 17,500 feet, considerably lower than usual. Our IP[22] was over the channel and our target area was only a few minutes inside of the coast. A fair amount of flak was coming up ahead of us, but we turned before we encountered much of it. The bombs really blanketed that area and guns that had been firing at us were apparently knocked out or discouraged, as the group behind us didn't have anything shot up at them.

After we dropped our bombs we made a sharp turn to the right and Roy was able to get a good look at the results. The whole area was bursting with bombs. We carried 52 100-pound general purpose bombs and so, with all of the heavies concerned, there were thousands of bombs dropped there.

On returning to the base we found the ceiling was 900 feet, but it wasn't a bad deal because over the channel it was fairly broken and we came in individually underneath the clouds. Landed at 10:00. One of the best missions I've been on. Some ships suffered flak holes and at least one crew had a few wounded crew members.

July 19th, 1944

The boys returned from a mission to Saarbrucken, Germany around noon. We sent out only 24 ships and none were lost. Lately we have had several buzz bombs[23] land in the vicinity. One buzzed overhead this noon.

July 20th, 1944 – MISSION #10 – 6:10 hours

Today, on our tenth mission, we visited Germany for the first time. Our group has had missions there on several different occasions (only yesterday for one), but it was our first taste of it.

Our whole group had been put on alert last night and this morning about 02:00 the CQ came and got Charlie and Juvie up so that they could attend the special lead crew briefing. This is rather unusual for a wing crew so I figured we might be flying in a deputy lead position. This later proved to be true. About a half hour later Kolloff and the rest of us were routed out for an early morning breakfast before briefing at 04:00.

Our target was the factory at Ruesselsheim, near Frankfurt, which is one of the three factories in Germany building flying bombs. It was formerly one of the largest automobile

---

[22] Initial Point: the start of the bomb run

[23] V-1 bombs were unmanned flying bombs programmed to fly to London and explode. They flew low.

factories in Germany and was supposed to be quite important – besides, we all have a personal grudge against the flying bombs which have been bothering us lately.

The 8th Air Force was going out in considerable strength and ours was just one of the ten different targets being hit in Germany today. Our group put up 36 airplanes. We were the deputy lead for the low squadron led by Capt. Aubry. Capt. Hector, our squadron operations officer, flew in the co-pilot's seat and Roy flew as a waist gunner and enjoyed the scenery.

We didn't take off until about 07:30 so we enjoyed daylight the entire time. The ship assigned to us (475 – a B-24J) was a good ship and didn't give us any trouble except for a leaky gas cap which caused some gas to siphon out for a while after takeoff. We were carrying a full load of gas (2800 gallons) and ten 500-pound demos[24]. The lead squadron carried a mixed load of demos and incendiaries. We used the regular instrument ascent to assembly altitude at 15,000 feet and I tried to stay on the ball as Capt. Hector was along. It was the first time I have had someone other than the regular crew. The assembly went off ok although large B-17 formations kept cutting across our buncher.

After leaving the English coast around 09:30 we started our climb to 20,000 feet which we attained as we reached the coast of Holland at 10:00. About this time we began encountering prop wash from the groups ahead of us, although it wasn't as bad as some times. It, plus the wide varying airspeeds of the leader, kind of threw me off and some of us didn't fly the best of formation for a while. P-47s[25] joined us here and escorted us in the rest of the way, zig-zagging back and forth above us and beneath us. By the time we had reached the IP we were at 23,000 feet. We had about a six-minute run to the target and during this time we were all able to see much too plainly a box barrage of flak over the target area. It really looked black ahead with the puffs of flak bursting. I was kept busy flying the plane so I didn't have so much time to worry about it. I was also bolstered by the fact that the ship was equipped with heavy bullet-proof glass in the cockpit. This little feature always helps my morale![26]

We dropped our bombs ok, and with the flak bursting around us quite a bit we made a pretty sharp turn off of the target and got the hell out of there. No more accurate flak was encountered and the trip home was rather uneventful. We landed a little after one o'clock.

Upon landing we counted only four flak holes and we decided that the ack-ack wasn't so accurate considering its intensity. Later we learned that the lower section of our squadron didn't fare so well and that they were pretty well hit. Kolloff and Lee both got quite a few

---

[24] Demolition bombs that explode in all directions
[25] American pursuit fighter plane: P-47 Thunderbolt
[26] Of course, with any close explosion it wouldn't matter because the whole plane would be blown up.

hits and Murphy had his hydraulic system shot out and landed at Woodbridge. Woodbridge is a special base because it has a really long runway.

Wright's crew fared the worst and their nose gunner is in danger of losing his arm. He was hit over the target and got a hole knocked in his shoulder as big as a fist. Apparently Lt. Sheppard, their bombardier, did a pretty good job of giving him first aid. Lt. Wikenhauser of our squadron had to drop out of the formation and finally had to ditch after losing two engines. Air-sea rescue picked him up and he will be back here soon. The bombardier was killed and two gunners are missing. The other seven made it ok.

Photographs of the bombing show that our group did some good bombing and should have knocked that plant out for some time.

July 24th, 1944 – MISSION #11 – 5:15 hours

Today we intended to do big things but due to the weather the heavies didn't accomplish much. About the only thing we can say is that got another mission in and it was an easy one at that.

We had a good night's rest to start with as they didn't brief until 07:45. Briefing was unusually brief as our takeoff time was at 09:30. Just about the entire 8th Air Force was to blast away at the Germans in preparation for an attack by the Americans ten miles southwest of St. Lo.

We led the high element again and were in the lead squadron. We had to climb through an overcast about 5,000 feet thick and I believe I sweated it out more than the rest of the mission. We assembled at 15,000 feet and flew the rest of the mission at that altitude (the lowest of a mission so far). They didn't expect much flak so it was ok to go in at this level. While crossing the channel we were encountering a solid undercast and many of the groups were being recalled. Fortunately we were allowed to go on to the target, so we got credit for another mission. Some flak was encountered, but it was rather scattered and didn't come very close. Some ships did get shot up a bit though.

Some of the area was clear, but the target area itself was covered so we didn't drop our bombs. I believe the weather over here is Hitler's best ally. Got a glimpse or two of the Cherbourg peninsula as we flew over and then we skirted to the left of the German held Guernsey and Jersey Islands and headed for home. Let down over buncher 27 and broke out around 2,000 feet with the usual poor visibility and headed back to the field by ourselves. Our gunner Mason didn't go with us today as we needed only a crew of nine. The ball turret has been removed from the ships. Guess they don't figure it is worth it. It weighs better than 1,200 pounds. so that is quite something in itself.

July 25th, 1944 – MISSION #12 – 5:45 hours

This morning we were briefed for the same target as yesterday and this time we were able to drop our bombs (52 100-pound demos). Most of those who flew yesterday flew again today and in the same spot. I was still pretty tired from yesterday so I didn't like getting the high element lead again, as that puts all the work on the pilot.

Took off at 07:30 and had to climb through clouds, but it wasn't as bad as yesterday. As we approached France the weather began getting worse and we were authorized to drop down to stay under the clouds. We dropped from 15,500 feet to 11,500 feet – the lowest we have ever bombed – didn't even need our oxygen for a change. Fortunately there was very little flak and it wasn't near us anyway. Heavy flak really could have done some real damage at that altitude.

Forts and Libs[27] were all over the sky and the prop wash over the target area was pretty rough. There was some talk that the bombs were hitting short (of at least some groups), but our pictures showed 60% of the bombs dropped in the MPI (main point of impact). Our group was again commended for its good bombing, but the Colonel was heckled about our formation flying. I, for one, did about the best I could under the circumstances, but the major said I was flying too high. My wing men – two new boys (Shaw and Hill) did a poor job and everyone jumped on them. I guess both the lead and high squadron weren't so hot. At any rate we got our bombs on the target ok and that's what really counts.

July 27th, 1944 – MISSION #13 – 4:15 hours

At briefing at 02:15 this morning everything was quite secret and it looked as if something big was up. It almost looked to us as if there was going to be another Allied landing near the Calais area. Our target was a heavy gun emplacement three miles southwest of Cap Gris Nez. The target itself was supposed to be defended by 28 heavy anti-aircraft guns.

We took off at 05:20 and ran into numerous layers of clouds on our climb to assembly altitude – 23,500 feet. For a while we couldn't assemble, as our squadron leader, Capt. Conger, had a taxi accident and was late getting into the blue. Finally assembled on the deputy leader and Conger took over from there. It was about -28° C at that altitude and I was glad to have my electric-heated suit. It made all the difference. We flew over the target area but weren't able to drop our bombs due to the blasted weather. We should have been able to drop something that they would have remembered us by as we were going to salvage our three ton load of 1,000-pounders. We had a little flak shot at us, but it wasn't close.

---

[27] B-17 Flying Fortress and B-24 Liberator

Landed at 10:00 after coming in in formation under the weather. We came in over the field around 200 to 300 feet. Was glad we had an easy position to fly, for a change. Roy was able to do some flying. We led the low element. Until we flew this mission, we called it twelve-B. Now that it is over we call it number thirteen.

July 30th, 1944

Today was a lazy day for me. It was raining hard most of the afternoon and we just loafed around. Slept some in the afternoon and did some reading. Wrote letters in the afternoon and evening.

Bill Aloan, Kolloff's co-pilot, got home in the morning and had quite an experience. They lost an engine (number four) over the channel and went on to the target near Paris and dropped their bombs. Then they lost the number three engine and headed straight for home with four P-47s escorting them. They threw everything overboard including guns and flak suits. Just when they sighted the coast, the Germans opened up with a lot of flak. They were only at 6,000 feet and so they were really sprayed even though they did take evasive action (which was quite something with two engines out on one side). The fighters kept out of the flak but kept calling encouraging remarks over the radio. The radio operator was hit in the shoulder but didn't bleed much and kept on working. Bethune was hit in the cheek by a piece of glass but wasn't hurt. The P-47s led them to their field, but they overshot that field and landed at a nearby Polish fighter field. The Poles were quite friendly and wanted them to stay and drink beer. They really like the P-51. Sure glad Bill made it back ok. He is lame from pushing on the rudders.

July 31st, 1944

This morning, about 04:00, we were all awakened by a roaring noise and a buzz bomb passed over very low. It really must have been close because it woke us all up and set up quite a vibration with its roar. It sounds like a ten ton truck without a muffler. We expected the darn thing to pass through the barracks and blow up. I can see why it is so hard on the Londoners' nerves.

August 1st, 1944 – MISSION #14 – 5:15 hours

Today we went after the rocket installations[28] again. Each of the three squadrons had its own target. We were leading the high element of 'B' squadron and our target was just north of Rouen.

We briefed at 07:00 and were scheduled to take off at 10:00 but it was 12:00 before takeoff

---

[28] Locations where rockets were fired, usually from a mobile platform

due to the zero hour being set back. On takeoff we 'sweated out' a low overcast instrument ascent. We didn't have time to get well spaced on our takeoff leg due to the low ceiling and the fact that B-24s from another base were taking off and cutting in front of us. Later we learned that we almost collided with another plane before we broke out of the cloud layer. Mason said it clipped by us before he could warn us.

I remember this incident very plainly but what I don't remember, looking back after 70 years, was the specific timing involved in an instrument assembly. We were to fly one minute after takeoff, then make a 90° climbing right turn toward the buncher. We were still in that first heading when out of the fog a ghost B-24 cut directly in front of us. I believe that pilot was late to make his 90° turn. He was supposed to be 30 seconds ahead of us on takeoff and he should have been out of our way. It all happened in a flash and I didn't have time to respond. If he had been five seconds later we would have had a terrible mid-air collision, but fate intervened.

We assembled at 22,000 feet and everything went pretty well until we tried to drop our bombs and couldn't due to mechanical trouble. We couldn't even salvo them with the emergency release. Later learned that one of the bomb bay doors hadn't fully opened and caused the trouble.

Didn't encounter any flak near our formation but Charlie saw some rockets coming up from Rouen as we turned at the IP. At any rate they didn't bother us. Landed about 17:00. Our bombing wasn't very effective according to the strike photos.

August 2ⁿᵈ, 1944 – MISSION #15 – 5:00 hours

This afternoon we were again sent against the rocket installations in France. Our target was close to yesterday's: St. Georges Sur Fontaine. This time we were flying a wing position for a change and we were really in the 'purple heart' element. We were the number twelve man in the low element and carried long delay fuses and a camera. As it turned out it wasn't a bad deal, as we took off last and didn't have to sweat out the instrument ascent and descent with the other planes. The weather was bad until we got over by London. It was clear from there on and we were able to drop our bombs ok. Once again our bombing results weren't so good. These rocket installations aren't very large and seem to be hard to hit.

We didn't encounter any close flak but the 490ᵗʰ group was rather battered by it. We could hear over VHF that a B-24 had had its rudders and oxygen system knocked out and the crew finally bailed out. American fighters were watching over them and we could hear the fighters talking between themselves and counting the parachutes as they came out of the plane. All nine got out ok.

We were able to leave the formation early because we were camera ship and were thankful for that. We flew under the 'scud' at about 500 feet and by the time we reached the vicinity of the base the visibility was very poor and it was getting late. We burst out near the field at only a couple of hundred feet and I really racked the old 24 around like I never had before because I didn't want to risk going around again. Rather proud of myself, but it was a little violent – didn't know if I would make it myself – gave the gunners a thrill. Later the rest of ships came milling in out of the soup. It is almost a wonder that they didn't have a collision or two.

August 4th, 1944 – MISSION #16 – 6:00 hours

Today's target was in Germany for a change. We enjoyed good weather and so the 8th Air Force was sent into Germany in strength. Our target was an oil refinery near Heide, Germany, on the Danish peninsula, called Hemmingstedt. In many ways it was an ideal mission.

We took off about 11:00 and assembled at only 6,000 feet which is a lot better than doing it at high altitude. We climbed on course until we reached our bombing level of 15,000 feet. We were leading the low element of the lead squadron led by Lt. Col. Fitzgerald and had a pretty easy time. For a change the whole group flew good formation all the way. Practically our entire time was over the North Sea.

We had a good bomb pattern, but our squadron's bombs fell short for the most part (at least partly due to broken clouds drifting over the target). 'B' squadron made a second run and did fair while 'C' squadron bombed the secondary target -an airfield at Ausum - with good results. We were almost expecting to run into some German rocket fighters, but no opposition was encountered - not even any flak. Charlie took Roy's place as copilot for a while on return and got a little formation time in. He didn't do too bad and really liked it.

August 6th, 1944 – MISSION #17 – 5:30 hours

This morning we went back to our old stomping grounds - the rocket coast. Our target was a rocket installation at Mont Cauvaire.

We briefed at 06:00 and took off at 09:00. We assembled at 24,000 feet and it was plenty cold up there as I didn't wear my heated shoes. We were leading the low element of the lead squadron. For some reason our group didn't fly very good formation - probably the high altitude didn't help. Had several aborts too. We had to make two passes at our target due to the clouds drifting over the area and felt rather conspicuous, as the old flak was coming up at us at a pretty accurate altitude. Then we had to make the second run and, to our surprise, didn't get as much flak this time, but of course it was a shorter run. Fortunately it wasn't heavy and we weren't hit. Had a pretty good bomb pattern, but our lead bombardier didn't do a good job and so we didn't do so good again.

August 8th, 1944 – MISSION #18 – 4:30 hours

This morning we tried our hand at the rocket sites near Rouen again. Ours was called Saint-Jean-du-Cardonnay and we bombed it by sections of six planes instead of the usual squadron of twelve. Guess we did a little better than some times, but not as well as we wanted.

We briefed at 06:30 and took off around 10:30 in a ground fog which had pretty well dissipated by that time. We drew lead of the high element again, but everything went along alright and it wasn't so bad. Had an unusually short mission because we didn't go the long way around London this time on our return. We were not bothered by flak. All that we saw was off in the distance. Really an easy mission.

After early chow we enjoyed a sun bath and later a shower. The war news of the American drive in France sure looks good.

August 11th, 1944

This morning we were awakened at 06:30 so that the crew could have some B-17 transition time. By the time we took off it was after 09:00. We, I guess I should say I, tried to take off, as I never made it on the first try. On takeoff I tried to jockey the throttles after the ship started off to the left, and after careening from one side to the other I finally ran off the runway to the right on the dirt. We didn't get stuck and I gave her a little power and taxied back to the handstand. There we found I had sheared the lock bolt (shear pin) on the tailwheel, but otherwise it was ok. After about fifteen minutes I took off again and made it ok this time. It was my first accident and was kind of embarrassing for me, but nothing was said. I think that the different style throttles on the B-17 were mainly what screwed me.

My problem was that I decided to handle the throttles by turning my hand over instead of from top, as in the B-24. But this was a mistake and I was awkward as hell. I never tried that again. But hey look at it this way, it was my only accident so far, and shear pins aren't very expensive.

August 12th, 1944

This morning we were awakened about 02:00 and were supposed to test hop our ship because of the darned bomb bay doors not opening properly. We got all ready to take off and found out that we had been supposed to climb to 23,000 feet to drop the bombs. We couldn't so we came back to area after early lunch.

Just after we got back Cpl. Ford said I was to fly on a practice mission sometime in the afternoon. I was so tired and disgusted I said to hell with it and Roy and I took a blanket and went out in the area back behind the barracks and took a sun bath and kept out of sight. Before long Charlie and Lt. Lee joined me, and Roy went to the show. They called over the loudspeaker for Lee and I, but we ignored it. I figured they could get someone else. Well to make a long story short we goofed off all afternoon and about 17:00 a call from operations reached us. Capt. Hector wanted to know why I didn't fly. I told him that I hadn't wanted to and then Col. Fitzgerald took over and demanded an explanation.

"We aren't running a Boy Scout camp," he said. "This is serious business." It didn't help that Fitzgerald was a West Point graduate.

I didn't have an explanation and he said for me to see him in his office at 09:00 tomorrow. After supper we had a meeting of all first pilots of the squadron. The meeting was about filling out some B-17 questionnaires and the major also said that a few pilots (in fact two out of 36) didn't show up for a practice mission, and we would have to go whether we wanted to or not – how true!

Shortly after Lt. Col. Fitzgerald hung up I got another call. It was from one of the enlisted men at Operations. Apparently he had listened to the conversation and he said he wanted to congratulate me. He said he had never heard someone do what I did and not try to make an excuse or blame someone else.

I said, "Thanks, I guess…" I could have told them that they were the ones I was ticked off with for choosing me so often, which they admitted doing because I was usually close by and it was easy to notify me, but it was too late for that. The fat was in the fire, so to speak.

Later Lee and I and Collings went with Major Sianis and a Capt. Carter went with his CO - Major Orban. We were called individually before Col. Fitzgerald and the two Majors to state our case. In my case the Col. said he couldn't understand why I suddenly decided to pull such a stunt and said it was direct disobeying of orders and said the major would have to press charges.

The Capt. and I will get a court martial. Lee will get company punishment and Collings is scot-free. They both had excuses. I was so scared I could hardly talk. Sure feel low tonight.

August 13th, 1944 – MISSION #19 – 5:15 hours

Today we had a 'blitz' mission, more or less, as we didn't have time to eat breakfast before briefing at 06:30. Later on the takeoff time was delayed about an hour, so we weren't so rushed after all, but of course we still didn't get to eat. I hate it when we don't get to eat.

We took off about 04:30 on runway 00[29] and made an instrument ascent through numerous layers and patches of clouds up to about 10,000 feet. It was just as well with me that we didn't have it right down on the deck as it gives you a better chance to get an interval, if the ceiling is up a couple of thousand feet (as it was).

We were leading the low section of the high squadron and we had our own bomb sight for a change, due to the unusual set up for bombing on this mission. We were to bomb a road intersection and each individual element of three ships had an independent bomb run. The whole 8th Air Force was out in strength bombing the Germans in France -- heavies were all over the place and the weather was good over the target area except for a haze layer. However, we couldn't go above 17,000 feet if we wanted to bomb visually. We bombed from 16,000 feet. Everything went well until we reached the approximate vicinity of the target, but Juvie couldn't find the target. It was certainly too bad. He spotted it when we were right over it but it was too late to drop then and we finally dropped on a secondary road.

Charlie navigated us around the flak areas on our way out and he did a good job. We didn't see much flak, but I saw more rockets than I had ever seen before. They don't look too accurate but they really look wicked. The rockets leave a zig-zag trail of smoke from the ground on up to where they explode, determined by the prevailing winds. There is more of an air of mystery about them, a bit spooky. None of our planes were lost, but we saw a B-17 explode in a group off to our right. Landed about 15:30 -- a pretty good mission all in all.

---

[29] Runway numbers based on geographical direction: 00 is north

On return to the area we learned that Capt. Flynn (Group Adjutant) wants an explanation from all officers on our crew for not flying yesterday. Happy day! Ugh!

August 15th, 1944

This morning I went over to see Capt. Flynn at 08:30. He said he was the officer appointed to investigate my case and wanted to explain what privileges and rights I had as well as letting me read the charges against me. I am charged with the 96th Article of War I believe – being absent after being alerted to fly. Apparently that isn't as bad as the way Col. Fitzgerald put it (violation of a direct order) as under that I could be given a dishonorable discharge, etc. The way it stands I might be court martialed or be given a reprimand plus restriction and/or fines by the Major or a general up at Division Headquarters. I looked over the charges against me – or rather the various testimonials. Charlie's statement wasn't as well worded in my favor as Roy's was, although it doesn't make much difference. One thing that is in my favor is a statement by Major Sianis saying I had been performing my duties in a superior manner and he rated me in the top 25% of his squadron. I knew if it was up to him I would get by ok. It will be about a week before I find out the results.

No trace of Lt. Wofford and his crew has been heard since the mission today. So far he hasn't been heard from. He may have landed in France ok though.

August 16th, 1944

Slept in as late as I wanted. Roy and I went to lunch around 11:30 and I spent all afternoon loafing around until 16:00 when Kolloff and I went to a meeting for all 1st pilots by the Colonel. They gave a critique of the mission to Germany today and then the Colonel told us first: that the B-24s would be out of here in a week and second: that we would have to go 35 missions now, and then we could go home and wouldn't have to come back. It means we will be here longer, but it is good not to have to come back.
Juvie got back from London in the late afternoon. He had gone to London with Capt. Hector and the Capt. had said he couldn't understand how I had screwed up. He said I had been under consideration for promotion to captain. I really screwed up. I sure regret it now and feel bad about it. Wrote to the folks this evening about it. Such is life – phooey!

As time went by I realized that Major Sianis didn't want to punish me, but with no excuse they had to do so. He would have preferred to have given me company punishment, more like a slap on the wrist, which would have done the job because I had realized what I'd done.

Lt. Woffard's crew still hasn't been heard from. They moved them out of their hut, so I guess they are MIA[30].

Today we had another mission to France but it was anything but a milk run - in fact it was our worst mission any way you look at it.

We were flying the number three position on the left wing of the 'B' squadron leader who in this case was Lt. Glaze. It was his first mission as a G-H pathfinder[31] lead and it also turned out to be his last. Capt. Alexander was the lead G-H ship in the lead squadron.

Our target was an airfield near Roye, France. It was supposed to be used by German fighters and we were to posthole the field by dropping numerous bombs on the runways, but that was only temporarily effective. We took off at 06:35 on time and made a regular climb and assembly at 17,000 feet. We climbed on course to our bombing level of 21,500 feet and everybody was flying pretty good formation. Our squadron was following the lead and on the way to the target we skirted several flak areas which shot up a little flak at us. Until we got pretty close to the target it didn't do any damage. As we approached the target we could see the flak coming up fairly thick (also a few rockets were adding to the fun). Most of it was falling behind the lead squadron, but apparently that enabled them to zero us in (as we soon found out).

We were just about ready to drop our bombs when all of the sudden – bang! The lead ship, Lt. Glaze, received a direct burst in the tail and the whole tail section blew up in a huge sheet of orange flame. The rest of the ship nosed down and disappeared from our view. For a few seconds after the blinding explosion we continued to fly off the left wing of the stricken B-24. It was as if the entire tail section had been chopped off of the fuselage. The interior of the fuselage is sprayed pea green, the gunners were gone, the guns were gone, like they'd been sucked out in the explosion. Then the 24 plunged violently down toward the ground. There was no escape and all of the crew were lost. It was a sad ending to our B-24 flights in England. It was such a shock to us that none of us could talk for a minute and then we all tried to talk at once.

The deputy lead, Capt. Johnson, pulled up in position and so we were on his left wing. He dropped his bombs right away and we dropped ours then. Later we learned that due to a blunder he didn't have a bomb sight and he dropped his bombs early. About that time we didn't worry about hitting the target anyway. Planes and flak were all over the place. Our squadron broke up like a covey of quail. Those direct flak hits are rough. Lt. Brown, a

---

[30] Missing in Action. Later we learned that Lt. Brad D. Woffard was a prisoner of war.

[31] A ship that is equipped with a radar and can guide you through bad weather or clouds

good boy, was riding in the tail turret of Glaze's ship. No doubt he never knew what hit them. Capt. Sierks had a chance of getting out, but it is doubtful if they made it. One ship, Lt. Washington's, had its whole number two engine and prop knocked completely off and he peeled out of formation. He hasn't been heard from since. A fighter pilot reported that nine chutes came out of the plane, so they should all be ok.

We held our breath and followed Capt. Johnson to the Rally Point where he intercepted 'A' squadron. By that time we were out of the flak and we breathed a sigh of relief. We were the only plane that stuck with Johnson, and we both flew back along with the lead squadron and managed to stay clear of the flak areas. It certainly was good to see the channel again.

When we were ready to land, the ship ahead of us on the approach cracked up on landing. It was Lt. Hastings, a replacement who cracked up just the other day. He had better throw in the towel. He did have his ship damaged, however, and so I guess he can't be blamed. The runway was then changed to 25 and the next fellow also cracked up when he came in with three engines. What a mess! About that time we discovered our tire had been hit by flak so we were instructed to land at the long emergency strip at Woodbridge in case we had a blowout.

We landed there ok. I guess the tire was ok because I landed rather hard. It was cut down to the fabric in a couple of places but they were small so we took off again and landed at our own field. We discovered approximately a dozen flak holes in various places – waist, nose, rudder, fuselage and wings. Fortunately nothing was serious.

Wager thought we had blown up and we thought he had been damaged, but we both came through ok.

August 21ˢᵗ, 1944

Today was damp and drizzling all day. Got a haircut and my rations[32]s up in the afternoon. Also filled out the long B-17 questionnaire, which was sort of an accomplishment by itself. The weather has been so bad that no one has been flying the last few days. Got ambition and washed my hair and a shower in the evening.

We were issued rations probably weekly to supplement our food. Sometimes we couldn't make a meal and would miss it and they were just a condensed thing, but it was

---

[32] Rations (or k-rations) were supplement bread and cheese or potted meat with crackers.

helpful.

I had Mom mail me some tea bags. We'd sit around at night sometimes if it was cool or chilly and heat up some of our rations and have our tea. The newspaper back home, the Missoulian, heard about it and thought it was pretty funny that she was sending tea to England for me.

August 23rd, 1944

Slept in late again and felt rotten - have been getting too much sleep I guess, and everything has been so dull around here.

In the afternoon we heard a talk by four crew members of the Lt. Diggs and Kaplane's crew who had bailed out over France and made their way back out. They had interesting stories to tell. Spent most of the rest of the afternoon loafing around and did some mail censoring to help Juvie.

Uncle Walt (our squadron adjutant) brought me an order put out by Col. Helton. I had the choice of a court martial or the 104th Article of War. I took the latter, which will probably result in a fine and reprimand.

Will probably be able to fly a little B-17 formation in the morning with Gillette and Meyers. Roy is in town, but Kolloff is going to fly with me. He is pretty eager – a good laddie.

August 24th, 1944

Got up about 05:40. Roy and Juvie were back, so Roy got up with me instead of Kolloff. Our takeoff was delayed until 08:30 because of the formation getting ready to take off for the mission. It didn't matter anyway, as the number three booster was out so we didn't get off.

Managed to get a ride on the liberty run[33] but just missed the train to Norwich[34] and had to wait until 15:00. Got to Norwich around 17:00 but couldn't see any trace of the liberty run to the base. The military transport advised me to take a local train to Attlebridge - which was supposed to be adjacent to the field. After considerable questioning I finally found it just in time and reached Attlebridge at 18:00. There I soon found out that it was only a

---

[33] A free ride between town and the base
[34] My friend Jay was stationed near Norwich.

station and was several miles from the field. Got a ride part way on a truck and then started to walk just as it started raining cats and dogs. Stayed under a tree for half an hour but still got my pants and shoes soaked. It was a good thing I had my raincoat.

Finally got a truck ride right to the base and then got a jeep to take me to headquarters. They didn't have any information there and it was pretty late anyway, but I was told to try the club. Got a ride there and the club officers informed me Jay had gone home and had left there about a week ago! Nothing to do but go back to Norwich then and got a ride on another truck to a bus stop, where I caught the bus to the train. The train for Ipswich didn't leave until 23:30 but I decided to take it anyway, so after a couple hours wait I got on it ok. Arrived around 02:00 and was lucky to get the special liberty run truck back, which meets the last train from London. Wasn't such a hot pass for me.

August 26th, 1944

Slept late this morning. Kolloff and a bunch of the boys had to get up and fly the B-17 in formation. They also had to fly in the afternoon so they really got a workout – 9 hours. However, the B-17 really is a lot easier to fly in formation.

We haven't heard any more about going home so it probably won't pan out.

September 1st, 1944

Ah me. Much to my sorrow we were awakened about 08:00 for flying again. Briefing was at 09:30 for another blasted practice mission – only this one was special because it was to last over seven hours and we carried a 5,000-pound bomb load in addition to the full gas load of 2,700 gallons. Roy went on sick call because of a cold so we had another co-pilot, Lt. Neal, Winingers's co-pilot. He seems to be a pretty good boy, but I did most of the flying. We took off about 11:30 and landed after 18:00. A full day. We flew the lead of the third element again. Went up to 23,700 feet but ran into clouds, so we finally turned back from our scheduled cross-country and spent the rest of the flubbing around closer to the field. Hit the sack early.

September 4th, 1944

Today the group was on stand down so nobody flew. The weather probably would have prevented it anyway. We are supposed to be operational now and as soon as we get some good weather we may get some more missions in. I hope so.

Got a letter from Major General Partridge today and he severely reprimanded me and fined me $80.00. Half of one month's base-pay. Could have been much worse I guess, but it still isn't good.

September 7th, 1944

This morning I awoke to find that it was raining cats and dogs, so I slept in even later than usual. It continued to rain hard all afternoon and so I stayed in the barracks and loafed. In the evening I wrote a letter to the folks and learned that we were to fly a combat mission tomorrow morning. There are eight crews from our squadron and everyone in our barracks is flying, including the two new replacements (on Lt. Miller's crew). They are kind of excited about it all, as it will be their first mission. It is something new for us too, as it will be our first mission in the B-17. Haven't had day-combat for some time now either.

Juvie got his promotion today to first lieutenant!

Sept. 8th, 1944 – MISSION #21 – 7:15 hours

For the first time in three weeks we finally managed to get in another mission – this time in the big, single-tailed bird – the B-17.

We briefed at 04:30 and took off at 07:30. Our group was putting up a full thirty-six ships plus three spares, and our spot was leading the third element of the high squadron. The heavies were out in pretty good strength with targets in western Germany. Our target was apparently pretty important as ten wings or upwards of four hundred heavies were assigned to it. It was a large ammunition dump at Mainz, Germany, and it was defended by one hundred flak guns.

Our assembly altitude over the buncher was raised to 15,000 feet at the last minute due to weather conditions. After we assembled, we climbed on course en route to the target. Our course took us over a large area of France, which incidentally had been liberated from the Germans since our last raid. It was comforting to know that the Germans no longer were down there ready to take a crack at us. We crossed France and a corner of Belgium and Luxemburg on into Germany. We were originally scheduled to bomb at 25,000 feet but we finally had to climb to 29,000 feet in order to get above the cloud layer.

As we turned at the IP, we could see a barrage of flak and rockets over the target area, but we passed through it fairly well. Some flak puffs were at our level, but it didn't get real close to our ship. Most of it went to the group just a little ahead of us and several thousand feet lower. That didn't make us jealous either and we were thankful for our extra altitude. We had trouble getting our bomb bay doors open and almost didn't get our bombs away. Our squadron didn't do so hot anyway as the leader had trouble with his doors also and as a result we hit past the target. 'A' squadron did pretty fair though, and I guess the target was pretty well beaten up by the day's end. The rest of the mission was uneventful and we landed at 14:30. Our first combat mission in the Fort (B-17) turned out to be much easier than it first looked. We got only one flak hole – a small one in the plexiglass nose near the bombardier's seat.

After interrogation and critique we enjoyed chow and then back to the hut and a hot shower. Felt pretty pooped as it was a long mission and a pretty full day.

Sept. 10th, 1944 – MISSION #22 – 7:35 hours

Our target today was an aircraft component factory at Nurnberg deep in central Germany. Takeoff was scheduled for 07:30, but we were delayed slightly by a blown spark plug in engine three. All of the plugs had been changed and they hadn't done a very good job on tightening this particular plug, and it came loose while running up the engine. Fortunately they were able to fix it in short order and it didn't hinder us except to delay our takeoff.

We entered the continent over the Dutch coast and continued over Belgium and on into Germany. We swung below Frankfurt and on to the IP. Flak and rockets were coming up in pretty good force over the target, but our squadron wasn't bothered by it much. We were leading the number four element in 'B' squadron and none of us were able to drop our bombs due to a mix-up at the IP. Targets were being hit all over the area and we were able to see an ammunition dump blow up nearby. As our squadron still had its bombs we continued on all by ourselves to bomb the last resort target, a chemical factory at Darmstadt. We didn't encounter much flak and came through unscathed, but we were glad to get back in the main bomber steam returning home. Guess we were lucky to have good fighter support.

Back to base at 14:30. It was a pretty long mission and wasn't too easy, although we weren't damaged. Brought back two incendiaries, which had gotten hung up in the bomb bay. Saw two B-17s go down but they weren't from our group.

Sept. 12th, 1944 – MISSION #23 – 6:45 hours

Briefing today at 03:45 disclosed that we were hitting an ordnance plant at Magdeburg, about 60 miles southwest of Berlin. We were supposed to lead the low element of the lead squadron, but at the last minute we were shifted to 'B' squadron due to a mix-up in the way the bombs had been loaded. Later we learned that this was certainly a lucky break for us.

Went up over the North Sea and entered Germany near Wilhelmshaven. We caught a little flak here and on our turn from the IP to the target, we saw the most solid wall of flak and rockets that we had ever seen. It really gives a fellow a sinking feeling. I was conscious of the fact that my legs were trembling slightly, but was too busy to think about it for long. From our position in 'B' squadron we saw two of our boys in 'A' squadron (just ahead of us) get hit hard by flak. One burst into flames and one spun down out of control. No one was seen to get out. It seemed as if we would never get out of the flak area and I kept thinking how old E.L. (Wager) and us would manage to get through ok. E.L. was on our left wing. Miraculously our whole squadron was still pretty well intact, but about the time we reached the rally point we heard 'C' squadron calling for fighter support as they were being hit by the Nazi fighters. Owens, our tail gunner, was able to see most of what happened, and it really was a terrible thing. Half of 'C' squadron was shot down – seven ships knocked down in a few moments, and most of the rest were badly shot up. Several landed at Brussels, one crash landed there. Lt. G. Brown, the only 862nd boy in 'C' squadron crash landed here. He really was hit hard. He had 200-300 holes. He had to feather[35] the number four engine and all of the props had large 20 millimeter and .50 caliber holes in them. His flaps, elevator, ball, and tail turrets were hit hard, and his tail wheel was blown off. He made a nice wheel landing and did a good job in bringing it back. Four gunners were wounded – his tail gunner will lose an eye. They believe they shot down three German fighters.

In 'A' squadron the two Bisaro brothers were flying on the wing of the high element leader. They are both first pilots and have their own crews. Edwin Bisaro was shot down over the target by flak and his older brother, Arthur Bisaro, saw him go down and called out, "There goes my brother!" It sure is hard on him[36].

Well, this was the first time our group was hit by fighters and it came as a heavy blow even though we knew we might get hit at any time. We lost NINE crews – seven to fighters and two to flak. Also had two ships crash land and had numerous other ships hit bad and suffering wounded. Most of the crews were in the 863rd squadron.

Wager and I just about got hit by the high element of the lead squadron when it crossed under us (even though I pulled up to the level of the 3rd element). What a hectic day!!

Sept. 13th, 1944 – MISSION #24 – 6:30 hours

They got us up again this morning for another crack at Germany. Our target was the I.G. Farben chemical factory (synthetic oil) at Ludwigshafen. The fact that it was defended by 150 guns didn't sound any too encouraging - especially after yesterday's rough mission. We briefed at 03:30 and it was still dark when we took off at 06:15 – the first night takeoff for some time. We had a pretty good spot leading the third element of the high squadron. We carried six 1,000-pounders. The whole 8th Air Force was out again today.

---

[35] A procedure to reduce drag on the propellers by rotating them so that the wind doesn't catch them. Used when the engine was off or not responding. It was activated electrically by a switch.

[36] As fate would have it only 23 days later Arthur was shot down on a mission to Munster on October 5, 1944, but he bailed out over Holland.

We went in over the French coast and started our climb to the bombing altitude – 25,000 feet. Crossed the battle line at the Moselle River and encountered little flak.

When we turned on the IP to the target we really started sweating it out. At first we saw no flak at all, but before long we saw it start coming up – but thick! As we got into it, it sure looked awful – we could see the orange and red flame bursts as the stuff exploded just ahead of us. As usual it seemed impossible to get through it but we managed to somehow, with only two flak holes. One hit Charlie's oxygen hose and knocked it out and gave him a start. Many of the ships from the other squadrons were hit pretty hard. Saw numerous engines feathered. Lt. Meyers and Bowden had to land at Brussels. One ship caught fire and some parachutes were seen to come out. I guess it was Lt. Donald Vandertill of the 861st, as he is missing[37].

Our hut mates, the navigator and bombardier on Miller's crew, were on their third mission and got over fifty flak holes. Their radio operator had a piece of flak go through the flak suit he was wearing and stopped only when it hit his .45 automatic which he was carrying in a shoulder holster. It undoubtedly saved his life, as he was hit just below the heart.

September 17th was the start of a four-day leave, and Charlie said he wanted to visit Cambridge University with me. So we caught a ride with a truck to Ipswich. It took about three hours to Cambridge and we arrive around 16:00. We got a cab to the Red Cross Officers' Club and got established there.

September 18th, 1944

Slept in fairly late today and then Charlie and I went window shopping in Cambridge. Later we walked around in the University buildings and grounds nearby the club. The grounds are beautiful and well kept. After lunch we rented a canoe for a couple of hours and cruised down the canal that flows through the campus and had a pretty enjoyable time.

I thought I should have more contact with the enlisted men and I would walk over to their quarters on Saturday mornings and visit if we didn't have something else scheduled. I believe they thought it was ok and it was always a friendly chat. You don't

---

[37] Later it was confirmed that he was killed in action.

have much training on being the commander and pilot of your crew, and some people were almost overly friendly with their crew, officers and noncommissioned, but I thought there should be some distinction between the officers and the enlisted personnel. Not to say that the officers were the lofty people, but I would call my fellow officers by their first name, but with the enlisted men I used their last name. They seemed to accept that and they thought I was a little on the formal side, but I think they knew I respected them and had to depend on them and the whole team had to be that way. Charlie and I, however, had our own system.

When Charlie and I went to Cambridge and had just started on the train he turned to me and said, "You know Bob, we need to have nicknames. I'll be 'Pinky' and you'll be 'Bugs'."

And from then on that's the way it was, though none of the others knew our code, which was just as well.

Sept. 19th, 1944

While we were on pass the group had a mission to Darmstadt, Germany and four flak guns knocked down two of our planes. Lt. Jacob Landerman (860th) had his ship hit hard and it blew up and broke apart. Capt. William C. Holman's (863rd) ship caught on fire after being hit and the whole crew is believed to have parachuted out over the front line[38].

Sept. 22nd, 1944 – MISSION #25 – 6:15 hours

Had our first mission for nine days today – our fifth mission in the B-17. Took off about 1,000 feet and climbed 'through the scud' (a thick haze layer) for about 5,000 feet. We led the fourth element in the lead group. Our target was a tank factory at Kassel, Germany which was supposed to be defended by ninety guns. We bombed at 25,000 feet and dropped a three ton mixed load of demolition and incendiary bombs. Fortunately the target was overcast and Jerry had to use radar to direct his guns on us. While they had a pretty good bunch of guns bursting at us, our chaff[39] must have thrown them off, as most of it was below us (although all too much was bursting around us). Most of us got by without many hits – we didn't get any. We sure are sweating out all of these missions these days!

---

[38] Later information confirmed that Holman was also killed in action.
[39] Bundles of tin foil strips released from an aircraft to confuse the radar detection

On our return we had to drop down to within a couple of hundred feet due to the terrible visibility (heavy haze). We finally landed after getting cut out of the pattern a couple of times. It sure isn't healthy with thirty six other B-17s milling around over the field. Our group didn't lose any ships, but we saw two B-17s from the group ahead of us (the 34th) collide and spin down and break apart.

September 24th, 1944

It was cold and raining this morning and it continued all day. We spent the afternoon in the barracks and certainly were thankful for the nice little fire in our stove. There is another rumor going about that some of us may go home early. Phooey! I would feel better about it if I had thirty missions in - that way I think we would get credit for a tour.

In the evening we saw the show "Princess O'Rourke" with Olivia de Havilland. Had seen it before, but enjoyed it again. Olivia certainly is a beauty too.

This evening we had a 'crash' alert. We all tore outside and we heard a roar in the distance. In a couple of moments a buzz bomb flashed by and gave us a real thrill. I have never been so close to one. It was only a couple of hundred feet from our barracks and I figure it was about 150 feet high and doing about 200 mph. It is quite a terrifying weapon. It was so close we could see the red hot exhaust stack as well as the flaming exhaust gases.

Sept. 26th, 1944 – MISSION #26 – 7:00 hours

Our target today was a large tank and armored car factory at Bremen, Germany. There were supposed to be 225 guns at the target area, but our route was designed so that they could not bring the full number of them to bear on us.

We had the best position in the whole group – lead of the number three element of the high squadron. We carried three tons of incendiaries and bombed at 26,500 feet. When we turned on the IP we saw a pretty heavy concentration of flak. When our group approached the target area we started evasive action and we did remarkably well. The guns in the target area seemed to be divided into individual batteries (more so than usual) so I guess this helped the cause. At any rate, we came through ok and avoided a lot of flak. We dropped our bombs visually although we didn't get to see the results. According to the photos we saw we didn't hit the target very well.

Everything went quite well on the return (which was almost entirely over the North Sea) except for the sun which was in our eyes and the fact that we let down dangerously close to the lead squadron for a while. We returned first and were number two to peel off – usually we mill around for half an hour before landing. Landed about 18:30 – a pretty fair mission.

September 27th, 1944

Had the usual lazy morning and spent the afternoon washing, etc. Went to the early show "Make Your Own Bed", a comedy with Jack Carson. It was fair.

The group went to Ludwigshafen again but we weren't on it. They bombed through the overcast so they weren't hit bad. One group of B-24s was hit hard by German fighters. About 44 heavies were lost so the opposition isn't dead yet.

Looks like old 'Colonel' Lee (Wright's co-pilot) is about 'shot'. He was on the last six missions (three in the last three days). This morning he passed out and was pretty pale looking. He is going to go to the flak shack[40] for seven days. It may be that he has flown his last mission.

Sept. 30th, 1944 – MISSION #27 – 6:15 hours

Our mission today turned out to be a pretty rough one for us although at first it seemed that it might be a fairly easy one. Our target was a railroad marshalling yard at Bielefeld in the German Ruhr. It was only supposed to be defended by twenty guns. We flew a wing position for a change – on Lt. Hogan's right wing. He led the third element in the lead squadron.

Our bombing altitude was lower than usual (23,000 feet) and as luck would have it we encountered a cloud layer just a few minutes from the target. It was a pretty poor situation as we had trouble even seeing our element leader at times, much less the lead ship. Just before bombs away we broke into a clear area and about that time I was able to see three planes (apparently B-17s) spinning down from some group several miles ahead of us and off to the left. I didn't have time to think about that very long because just about that time bombs were dropped and a tremendous explosion occurred right next to us. I was looking to the left, flying formation off of Hogan, but I was able to see an enormous sheet of orange flame out of the corner of my eye (to the right). At the same time our plane was hit by blast and fragments of the explosion.

The explosion was caused by the fourth element leader exploding. He really blew up in no uncertain manner. Roy saw it and it blew up into bits of flying debris. The largest things left were a couple of the engines which managed to stick together. It was really a wicked affair. Certainly they never knew what hit them. We later learned that his bombs had

---

[40] A nice housing area soldiers were sent to in order to help relieve them of the stresses and traumas of war

exploded. At first we believed the ship had been hit by rockets, but many claimed that a ship piloted by Lt. LaFlame in the high element had dropped his bombs on top of Treece's ship thus causing the whole plane to blow up. This is certainly a possible explanation due to the poor visibility just coming out of the clouds.

Right after that we had to dodge Lt. LaFlame's ship which had several of its engines and wing on fire. We were sweating him out as he was getting pretty close to us and we were expecting him to explode at any minute. After a bit he left us and several chutes were seen to be leaving the ship. Later reports indicated that the ship did burst into flames all over and explode.

In those few moments we also had other troubles. Charlie had been hit, our bombs hadn't dropped or released when they were supposed to, and number four engine had been damaged by the blast or concussion from the explosion. We did our best to keep up with our squadron, but our engine trouble and the weight of the bombs caused us to lag back. Juvie looked after Charlie, and Andersen went down to help him after Hanwell took over the top turret. As soon as Juvie was able to he went back to the bomb bay and kicked out the bombs over Germany. We don't know what we hit but we couldn't keep up with the formation with the bombs and we would have been duck soup for fighters.

Fortunately we had excellent cover by P-51s and P-47s. After we dropped the bombs we were able to catch up with the formation.

By this time Charlie was pretty well taken care of and Andersen stayed with him the rest of the way home.

A bomb fragment had hit him in the kneecap, possibly fracturing it, but he didn't lose much blood. Guess it scared him more than anything, but it was no laughing matter. The fragment had continued on through the nose and hit the number two engine and by this time it was losing a lot of oil and smoking. Number four was running a little rough and was only pulling 25 inches manifold pressure so we feathered it to see how we would do. Number two began to spout out so much oil that we unfeathered number four again. To our surprise it now pulled about 35 inches although it still was a little rough.

We sweated out the rest of the trip with the formation and then left it at the Dutch coast so as to get back early. We came back about 200 mph indicated and let down about 500 feet per minute most of the way. It seemed like we would never get back. Two P-47s escorted us part of the way.

There was one P-47 on each wing. We waved at them and they knew they were appreciated. I wish I had taken a picture of each one. Before we landed Roy started firing the flare gun off like crazy, but he was having fun. I was a little embarrassed. They must have thought that half the crew was dead and the other half wounded and here Charlie was just hit in the kneecap. It was here, however, that I made the smoothest landing ever. Charlie was injured and I wanted to make as smooth a landing as possible and I succeeded so well I hardly knew I was on terra firma!

About the time we reached the base we feathered number four as it caught on fire and was running rough as a cob. Number two wasn't in any too good of shape either as it must have been about out of oil. It was plenty nice to set her down on old terra firma and we taxied right over to the ambulances where the medics took Charlie out. He didn't seem to be in too bad of shape but didn't feel like smiling any. Poor Charlie! This was his 29th mission and he was going to quit on his 30th.

Thank you B-17! Losing an engine or two didn't faze you.

Our squadron (the lead) was the only one that was hit. We lost two crews – Lt. Treece, 860th Squadron and Lt. LaFlame, also 860th. Lt. Treece had 29 missions and was on orders to go home.

October 2nd, 1944 – MISSION #28 – 7:45 hours

Today our target was an airplane engine factory at Kassel which was supposed to be defended by 82 guns. The group was led by Lt. Col. Whitlock and we flew number three element lead in his squadron. We took off a little after 07:00. It was the first mission without Charlie. Juvie took charge of the nose with a spare gunner to help him man the guns.

Everything went normally until we got to the target area and then the lead ship wandered all over the area trying to pick up the target. We later learned that part of the pathfinder equipment had gone on the blink. Finally, when we did start on the run to the target, it lasted better than fifteen minutes, which seemed forever. The flak was right up with us bursting all around. We had some pretty close ones and got about six flak holes. Luckily no one was knocked down, but the lead ship had some good sized holes in it. Joe Jensen was flying number three position and I saw a burst of flak explode just below his ship just before bombs away. Don't see how it didn't get him.

It was almost 15:00 when we landed. Our right wing man claimed that a rocket barely missed our ship, but we didn't know anything about it. Couldn't tell much about the bombing results due to the clouds, but it is believed that we hit some railroad yards.

I saw one B-17 spinning down at the target from a group ahead of us.

October 3rd, 1944 – MISSION #29 – 8:00 hours

Today the 8th Air Force was concentrating on German airfields and accordingly we were to bomb an airfield that was supposed to have jet-propelled jobs on it. The field was located in southwestern Germany near Switzerland and it was called Kitzingen. It was a little unusual in one respect because there wasn't any flak expected over the target (although fighters were expected). It was to be bombed visually only, so for once we prayed for good weather. As luck would have it, the area was pretty cloudy so we bombed the secondary target, a marine engine plant at Nurnberg.

Luck was with us and although a fair amount of flak was shot up all around us, none of it came very close. Apparently the good old chaff did its work. We flew the very same position as the day before leading the low section of the lead group (led by Maj. Sianis). Also bombed from the same altitude (25,000 feet) and carried the same bomb load (ten 500-pound demos).

It was the longest mission we have been on and we were able to see the Swiss Alps on our return out of Germany. Had a lot of prop wash all day and we ran into scattered flak well after we thought we were out of German territory. Apparently it came from the battle line.

All planes returned ok due to the inaccurate flak. Roy thinks he saw a twin engine (jet-propelled) German fighter lurking near a formation near the target. Our fighter cover was good, P-47s and P-51s.

October 4th, 1944

We got to sleep in again for a change and I sure felt better afterwards. In the afternoon I took care of various affairs around the base – got my gas mask checked, found my bicycle and went to awards section to see what the score was. They said that I would be put in for DFC[41] at the end of thirty missions, but didn't know whether I would get it or not due to the 104th which rather tied up credit for two missions.

Saw Hector and he wanted to know whether Roy was goofing off or not, but I didn't say much. Roy came back from the hospital after a trip there this afternoon and I guess the doctor apparently thinks there might actually be something wrong with Roy's back, so Roy might be able to quit with thirty missions. The bad news for the crew is that it still looks like we might have to do thirty-five missions. Lord I hope not! We just hope for some

---

[41] Distinguished Flying Cross

replacements to relieve us before then.

October 5th, 1944

Got up and took a shower this morning and got cleaned up to go visit Charlie in the afternoon. Juvie went to London but Roy couldn't go as he has to go to the 65th General Hospital again tomorrow to see about his 'aching back'.

I got a ride on the ambulance to the hospital. Left about 13:00 and arrived there about an hour later. Charlie is doing ok, but it isn't fun for him. He looks a little pale. Had a pretty good visit with him for about an hour and a half before I had to get back with the ambulance. While there, a few Red Cross girls came in and sang a few songs for the boys. Came back about 17:00 and spent a quiet evening except for a little buzz bomb activity. For a change the anti-aircraft defenses were really opening up and we saw a lot of tracers and flak going up. Saw several huge red flashes so apparently some hits were scored. Kolloff and Miller flew today. Bombed Munster, Germany. Lt. Bisaro is missing, but he may be ok.

October 7th, 1944

Didn't do much again today as this was the last day of our pass. Had a lazy morning and spent the afternoon doing a few odds and ends in the barracks. Spent the evening writing some letters for a change.

The group went to Mersberg today and they all said it was the roughest flak they had ever seen. Even so, no one was shot down. Several men were wounded and another navigator killed. Some planes were shot up, of course.

Roy found out why he hasn't been promoted. Hector didn't like the idea of Roy not wanting to get checked out in the B-17. Roy had a talk with the major. It still looks like 35 missions, darn it!

October 8th, 1944

This morning were awakened before 04:00 for briefing at 05:00. None of us were any too pleased to see that we are going after the same target as yesterday, Mersberg. It has 250 flak guns at the target and numerous other flak areas nearby. According to Wager and everyone else who flew there yesterday, it didn't seem possible that anyone could get through it. The sky was black with the smoke at all altitudes.

As luck would have it everything was delayed an hour (presumably due to ground fog) and then the mission was scrubbed. That was one mission I wasn't sorry to see scrubbed.

Everyone was quite happy about it.

October 10th, 1944

Got up early for another mission (to Hamburg) but just before start engine was ordered, the mission was scrubbed. Would just as soon have gone ahead with this one, although it could have been plenty rough.

October 13th, 1944

Nothing doing again today although the weather was better. Juvie and I went over to the 65th General Hospital to see Charlie. We rode over and back on the ambulance with a screwball driver. Charlie seems to be better and he gets up now and then with a wheelchair and crutches. He expects to go home by boat in another two weeks or so. He will be sent to a hospital near his home in Kansas City and will probably have to keep his cast on for another two months.

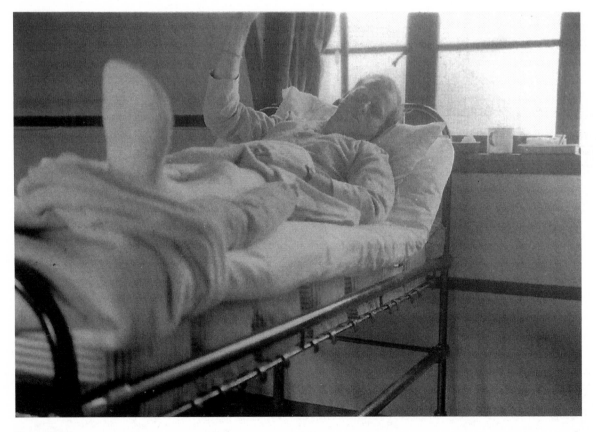

Poor Pinky

October 17th, 1944 – MISSION #30 – 5:15 hours

Today's mission turned out to be a little different in several aspects from the usual one. To start with, this was an early mission so we took off while it was still very dark. Briefing was at 02:30 and we took off about 05:30.

Our target was the marshalling yards at Cologne. There were supposed to be 400 guns at the target of which 220 were within range of us. Our group put up 42 airplanes. The regular 36-ship formation, plus six ships to fly as the low section for the low squadron of the 34th group. This small section of ships were all composed of 862nd boys and, as luck would have it, we were supposed to lead it. We had to have a navigator for this mission so Lt. Gleason flew with us. He is a good boy and kept busy all of the time. This was his thirteenth (or twelve-B) mission.

After we climbed to our assembly altitude it was still pretty dark and we began to have our troubles. Apparently our radio compass was being jammed by the Germans as we couldn't seem to get a very accurate bearing on our buncher. We got by finally, by using the G-box[42] and Gleason did ok with it. Finally managed to get a couple ships assembled on us before we hurried over to join the 34th at their buncher. By this time it was light enough to see what we were doing and the rest of our ships joined up with us ok. We in turn assembled with the low squadron of the 34th and from there, it was routine flying for us.

We bombed at 25,000 feet and dropped a mixed load of GPs[43] and incendiaries. The flak was pretty heavy, but we managed to get by with but two flak holes. One ship from the 34th was hit in one of the squadrons above us and it peeled out ahead of us. Came back in a hurry after leaving the 34th over the channel.

October 18th, 1944 – MISSION #31 – 7:30 hours

Today our target was Kassel and it turned out to be a long haul. We were supposed to fly the number two position in the third element of the lead group, but when we reached the assembly altitude our leader never showed up and we took over the deputy lead position. Our squadron then changed places with the high squadron.

Weather kind of screwed up a lot of the boys on the assembly and we were delayed somewhat by the time we left the coast. We finally climbed up to 27,000 feet due to the weather.

Had a pleasant surprise at the IP. I was beginning to sweat waiting for the flak to come

---

[42] Radar equipment
[43] General purpose bombs

up, but we dropped our bombs before I knew we had reached the target. Flak wasn't a problem today. Got shot at on the way back, but we reached friendly territory ok. About that time everyone was getting low on gas and so many peeled off and landed at emergency fields, though there wasn't anything left of the formation. We and a very few others decided we could make it ok and came back by ourselves.

I remember we were just humming along and the air was quite calm even though there was lightning in the distance. However, before long there was a buildup of static electricity and we experienced St. Elmo's fire and the tips of our propellers glowed with a bright blue light like a halo. It was really quite beautiful. It was the first time I had encountered it, but I was aware it could occur under the right circumstances.

Ran into a cloud black as coal on the way back over Belgium and got some 'gage time' (instrument time). It really was raining and we ran into several good rain storms along the way. Finally broke out near the coast and made it back ok to England. Juvie wasn't very sure of his navigation and we ended up over by Dover. By the time we got back to the base we were getting mighty low on gas – in fact a couple of tanks were nearly dry. Had about 140 gallons left according to the refueling men. When all tanks are full it comes to 2,800 gallons!

We were advised by radio that we could refuel at Brussels, but I thought they would expect us to get back if we could. I didn't even ask Andersen for a fuel check, which I ordinarily would have done. Andersen was our crew chief and engineer. He was my right-hand man while flying and I should have communicated with him more on this mission. That was dumb and very dangerous. How long would it have been before the engines began shutting down? Two or three minutes, or four or five? It didn't matter, we had landed at Debach.

October 25th, 1944 – MISSION #32 – 6:45 hours

Had my favorite spot in formation today leading the third element of the high group. Took off about 08:30 in a fairly thick fog.

Our target was an oil refinery at Hamburg. The area was defended by 250 heavy guns.

After a long run over the North Sea it was only about a half hour before we reached our target. Due to an accidental release by our leader, about one squadron dropped their bombs early, but that didn't stop us from motoring through the flak. Sure felt like waiting for the others outside of the flak area, but of course we couldn't. Quite a lot of flak and rockets were coming up, but it was pretty inaccurate due to the new chaff setup I guess. Apparently someone hit the target as a large cloud of dark smoke billowed up from the target area through the undercast.

Landed at 15:30, and after critique we had a real surprise from the colonel. He said we were through! Boy that was hard to take. Ha! Don't know when we will go home yet. Happy day! A real birthday present. My 22nd birthday.

Two years earlier, on my birthday, my brother had completed a mission to Le Harve, France. Two weeks after his mission, Bill had flown with the 48th Fighter Squadron of the 12th Air Force to Algeria to join in the invasion of North Africa.

October 26th, 1944

Had a pleasant day taking it easy and knowing that we had completed our tour. Went to the show "Fantasia" by Walt Disney in the afternoon. Rather a crazy affair and different to say the least. Spent the evening getting a few preliminaries taken care of for getting my footlocker packed. Also wrote home the welcome news. I know Mother and Dad will be happy. To bed at 23:30.

October 27th, 1944

Took it easy in the morning and this afternoon I went over to the hospital to see Charlie and took him the rest of his clothes. He is ok and expects to leave before long and fly back to the good old U.S. via C-54. He gave me a drawing he had made of the Ludwigshafen mission. He is coming over to the base tomorrow on a 24-hour pass.

Got back around 17:00 and went to chow with Kolloff and boys shortly afterwards. Spent the evening fooling around doing a little more packing and a little writing. Also had a bull session with Andersen and Hanwell and showed them my pictures.

This morning Kolloff and the boys had to get up in the early morning hours and be ready for a mission. Boy it was sure nice to be able to stay in the sack. Later the mission was scrubbed due to weather.

October 28th, 1944

Didn't do much today. Slept in late and turned in some equipment in the afternoon. Charlie came down for the party. I had several drinks at the club and got to feeling pretty good, said goodbye to buddies.

October 29th, 1944

Another rainy day and I didn't seem to do much. Got orders and a few clearances in the afternoon. Said goodbye to Charlie. I will miss him. Saw the show "Tender Comrade" with Ginger Rogers in the evening. Also went to church. Our enlisted men were throwing a drunk this evening and were feeling pretty gay. I guess they are entitled to cut loose some now. This is my last diary entry.

After saying farewell to Charlie and other crew members, Roy, Juvie, and I, as well as two or three other crews that had finished their missions, left by rail for Liverpool on the west coast of England. There we were to await our shipping orders back to the United States.

It was around the first of November. Liverpool was a cold, chilly area by the waterfront and tended to be kind of foggy. It was a rather gloomy place. We were housed in a large brick building while waiting to board ship for home. The rooms were very chilly and the hot water radiators were barely warm to the touch. I think I was cold the whole time there. We received orders from the 3rd Air Division when we first arrived stating that officers would have their luggage and canteens with a cup when we boarded our ship. So I decided to use my canteen right away for an unintended use where in the evening before bed I filled my metal canteen with the somewhat-hot water, put a towel around it, and placed it by my cold feet in bed. It helped a little but probably mostly was psychological in my endeavor to warm up a little bit.

We spent several all too long days and nights there, but I can't remember the food for some reason. We apparently had adequate food, and I don't remember being hungry. We were restricted to the immediate area and it was quite a letdown to be waiting around like that. I don't know how long we waited there, but it must have been at least a week or ten days, as it got to be quite a drag. We three officers weren't with any others that we knew and that didn't help matters. I don't remember any entertainment or news available.

As a result of being bottled up in close quarters with nothing to do, our bombardier, Juvie, had a knack for getting on people's nerves. He had kind of a feisty personality and he finally got on Roy's nerves. At one point they were ready to duke it out, so they went outside. I didn't bother going along, as I figured they'd had enough of me giving orders. They came back a few minutes later roughed up a bit and out of breath, but it did seem to settle them down.

Finally, we boarded a vessel manned by the coast guard and departed. It was the USS Wakefield, about 26,000 tons displacement, and it seemed to be a modern ship. Aboard the ship we had double bunks to live in and they were adequate, but of course it was all in fairly close quarters. We were escorted by a few smaller naval ships for the first two days or so, and in the most dangerous area for German submarines. After that we were on our own and the captain poured on the coal, so to speak. He was concerned about the subs and used a zig-zag heading to make us a harder target for the subs. Thankfully it was also a relatively fast ship and we didn't run into any problems of that kind in the journey.

The problem was the weather was stormy at the time, and the ocean was very rough for days on end. The pounding was hard on the ship and the crew said some seams in the hull had split open enough to be a concern. Two gun platforms for self-defense were also washed overboard. Some of the crew said it was the roughest trip they had ever been on. In addition to all of this, with the speed and the bouncing, the propellers would briefly come out of the water and vibrate as they picked up speed, which would shake the whole ship. This had an effect on me and for the first three days my stomach gradually became woozier, and although I never did 'feed the fishes,' I didn't feel very good. We didn't venture out on deck much, and if so only briefly, as it was very wind-swept. I am sure the enlisted men didn't fare as well, being located at a lower level with more crowded bunks and not as pleasant of dining facilities. But most importantly we avoided the German submarines.

Thanksgiving arrived about then and my appetite was beginning to come back. On the holiday they had an excellent meal of turkey, mashed potatoes, dressing and gravy with all the trimmings. I enjoyed it, but ate somewhat sparingly. Actually, the food was good for the whole trip, though I didn't get to taste much of it, especially at first.

Our journey across the Atlantic took about a week and ended at Boston. I was disappointed that we didn't get to see the Statue of Liberty when we came in, as we would have in New York, but it was still a joyous occasion. We went ashore in Boston and spent one night there in comfortable quarters. Our radio operator Hanwell looked us up and came over. We had a pleasant visit and then said farewell. I wish I'd kept track of him after our service, but good intentions don't count. Then Roy, Juvie and I were each separated by our geographical home destinations, and I was bound for the Northwest.

We were split into groups of about twenty returnees. When I got on my train, I sat down next to another first lieutenant. It was a surprise to meet Dean Greiner of Polson, Montana, and here I was from Missoula. Polson is a small town about 70 miles north of Missoula, situated on the southern shores of Flathead Lake, an area I was quite familiar with. He had been a B-17 pilot with a different group at a different location, but it was quite the coincidence. Our time on the train together was fairly brief, but we were involved with him many years later when my wife and I bought a piece of Flathead Lake property owned by him and his brother, but that's a later story.

I had flown over to England in May of 1944 and finished my missions on my 22nd birthday, October 25th, that year. It was such a relief to finally achieve that long sought goal not knowing whether you were going to make it through or not, and I was really relieved that we made it back in one piece.

Enjoying the sun with Juvie and Charlie

Bill Aloan (Koloff's co-pilot), me, Roy Walser, and Clyde Kolloff – Summer 1944

Part 5:

Life After the War

Back to the outdoors with the bear grass
In northern Idaho along the Lewis and Clark trail with my Honda Trail 90

Upon our return to the United States, most of the crew and I each received the Distinguished Flying Cross for accomplishing more than 30 missions as well as the Air Medal, which was for seven missions, with three oak leaf clusters each also representing seven missions.

It was great being home on a 30-day leave before Christmas and having survived air combat with the 8th Air Force. But we didn't talk about that, it was old news. I got together with Jay Lockhart a few times and met his younger sister Marybell, an attractive young woman. I also had plenty of time to print up a bunch of pictures I'd taken while I was over in England. I took them to the Missoula Mercantile where I had worked part time as a student. One of the places I'd worked was the wrapping and shipping department. My former boss in the department, Mina Thomas, was still there. She had been very nice to me and she and her husband had sent me a present or two while I was in England. At the Mercantile, Mina had a temporary helper there, a young woman that was helping during the upcoming holiday season. She took an interest in my pictures and when she spotted a picture of me en route to England as a pilot of a B-24, she took one look and said,

"Glamor puss!" And from then on that was my glamor picture.

There was a void in my life with Bill lost in the war and Ken Rigby drowned, but life goes on. During my remaining time home, Mom, Dad and I shared tasty meals with other families and relatives, but as usual the time passed quickly. I reported to Santa Anna, California by rail shortly after January 1st, 1945. The location was the former site of flying schools early in the war, but it was now where returnees from combat reported. Crews were coming back more and more from overseas for reassignment in the Continental United States area, including those from other theaters of war such as the Pacific.

While in Santa Anna I did get to visit with my dad's sister Rose and her husband Julian Clark. Their only son, Lynn, was on duty with the 8th Air Force as a bombardier on a B-17. His plane had been shot down by a Russian fighter pilot flying a YAK fighter over Russia, as they were preparing to land at the Russian base. The plan was to fly a long-range mission to Germany near Russia and remain overnight there with a small number of

B-17s. It was an absurd situation. Russia was an ally, but they had poor control over that fighter pilot. When the crew bailed out, two or three of the crew were killed during the encounter, but Lynn survived.

The Russians' only excuse was, "Oh, that pilot is crazy."

As might be expected, that plan was cancelled and never repeated.

Lo and behold my orders called for me to go back to Liberal, Kansas. It was kind of a letdown because it would have been nice to be assigned closer to the northwest, but there weren't many bases there. After spending a few weeks in Liberal my next assignment was to Lubbock, Texas for a six-week instrument course flying the single-engine Advanced Trainer (AT)-6. I didn't particularly enjoy the course, but it was good training. While under the hood was very tedious, you had to pay close attention to keep on course, as the AT-6 was pretty sensitive. All in all there wasn't much excitement, though a few times everything was shut down when a dust storm hit the area. Although my buddy Maury (Sal Mauriello from training) was there, I didn't see much of him, and it was back to Liberal in the middle of March. I was given a fifteen-day leave with five travel days back to Missoula.

I think the army was striving to keep us occupied. My next orders were to attend a four-engine instructor course from the 8th of May to the 22nd of June at Smyrna, Tennessee, near Nashville, right when Nazi Germany surrendered in Europe. The main flying tactic was centered on flying the B-24 with little power when landing, which required a steep descent because you'd drop like a rock in that heavy airplane. This was a non-glamorous assignment and the trouble was it took place in the summer. The hot temperature and the high humidity made it rather miserable flying. Typically we were assigned to report to the flight line at one o'clock, and all the while the B-24s had been baking out in the hot sun with all of the windows closed. It was very hot and we often did touch-and-go landings where we landed and rolled along, then hit the throttle to take off again, circled around, came back in, and did it again. The trick was to really cut the throttle at a higher elevation than usual when approaching the runway so the plane would sharply decline. If it wasn't done properly the plane would encounter a deadly stall where it just simply fell and crashed, so we had to be on our toes and really push the nose down in order to maintain a minimum flying speed. Making touch-and-go landings was definitely a workout, the sweat just really flowed. I wasn't sorry to graduate from that course.

Before I left for Liberal, I went to a Nashville night club with four other pilots for a little celebration for completing the course. We got a booth facing the dance floor and ordered a pitcher of beer. We never talked about combat, just BS and shot the breeze. I was enjoying the occasion when a lieutenant and a nice-looking brunette stopped at our booth.

The young woman pointed to me and said, "I'd like you to come with me."

I admit I was surprised, so I asked, "Would you like to join us here?"

That was not in her plans, because she repeated I was to come with her. Later on I wondered if she thought she had picked a dumb one, but I prefer to say I might have been a little naïve. Nevertheless, I quickly got up and forsaked my beer and buddies with no regrets. We walked over to a nearby table where the lieutenant, Fred, sat with his girlfriend, Fran.

My girl's name was Claire and the four of us departed for another location in Fred's car.

Too bad I couldn't have gotten together with my four buddies again so I could have said, "Hey guys, when Claire picked me that made me the pick of the litter. Bow wow!" Oh well.

Claire and I went to a cozy lounge and quietly sipped a couple of drinks while getting better acquainted. Afterwards we walked outside for a bit to Claire's residence. We went up to her apartment and then I became aware that Fred and Fran were in an adjoining room, but we proceeded into Claire's bedroom. Suffice to say I had a very pleasant evening and Claire showed me what real southern hospitality could be.

In the early hours I returned to the base with Fred, as I had already made arrangements to go back to Liberal. I would have liked to have seen more of Claire, pun intended, but that was not to be. So later on I was on my way back to good old Liberal on a Trailways bus. It was a tiring journey, a long day's ride, to return to the base.

Time passed and I was still at Liberal. I had met a captain from Pony, Montana, which was a little mining town southeast of Butte on the east side of the Continental Divide. He was a joker kind of a guy and was always laughing. He liked to call me junior because I was a lieutenant and he was a captain. Ken Marshall was his name, and he was a veteran from the Pacific and flew B-24s there. In my mind the pacific veterans were more apt to be captains because they stayed in one unit for longer periods, typically two years, whereas the European theater was six or eight months for most of us, or less than a year.

The headline when the news was announced at Liberal

When Japan surrendered on August 14th, 1945 I was at Liberal and there was quite a celebration, as could be expected. I was invited by a fellow pilot to go into town with him. He had a girlfriend who knew a girl who would be available for me, so I took him up on his offer and my girl Sal and I had a pleasant evening dancing as well as some hugs and kisses. Everyone was in a happy mood!

We were still in the army, however, and some of us received orders to report to Lubbock, Texas by September 14th for an instrument instructor school.

About a week later a first lieutenant, Marvin Rice, came up to me and said, "How would you like to ride with me? I've got my car and we can drive down to Lubbock."

I didn't know him very well, but it was fine. When we got there, the first thing we saw was these two gals driving in a car approaching us, and one had the nicest smile. She just lit up and I said to Marv, "She's for me!"

So we turned at the next corner, parked beside each other and got out and talked. The girl with the smile was Rae, and the other girl was Landa. We made a double date to get together that very afternoon and that led to a very nice and fun assignment there at Lubbock. Early on the four of us went on a picnic at a very small lake. There was no real established campground, and I thought later that it could have been a private little lake on a farm because when you flew over some of those areas in Oklahoma and Texas you'd see lots of little pothole lakes. We built a fire and had hotdogs and buns and marshmallows, as well as a little salad with olives and pickles. It was fun and we got to know the girls a little better, and I brought my camera along. They furnished everything and I trust we paid our way. We also went to a football game on one Saturday and to a little afternoon tea dance another time at the club. Rae was a classy girl.

After about three double dates, Marv showed up with a new girl, Betty, and it was plain to see that they really were sold on each other. Though she had been married before, they ended up getting married pretty quickly. It's odd that I didn't ever ask Rae on a date with just the two of us. She was very agreeable, everything was on the plus side with her. I think Rae would have liked to have gotten to know me better and the same for me, but

With Rae

fate had me aligned with a young Montana girl later on, so it was not to be. Marv was a little older than me and more sophisticated, more settled down, and willing to get married. I wasn't thinking about marriage, which was a good thing because I wasn't ready.

Our assignment in Lubbock only lasted about three weeks at the most. The army abruptly told us they couldn't guarantee how long we would stay active, but if we wanted to get out we would have to decide right away and would then be given orders to be discharged and go home. I was homesick for Missoula, and their uncertainty about how long we'd be required to stay in sounded very indefinite. If I was to stay, it was entirely at their convenience and they would tell us when to go. So I decided I would leave. Marv, however, chose to stay in.

After we separated and I had been back at home for a while, I got a letter from Betty saying that Marv had been killed in an airplane crash in New Jersey. He was a nice guy and I hadn't known him long, but he had been so agreeable and generous with me. It was a tragedy for them and so sad.

I got out in October of 1945 and planned to start winter quarter at the university with the goal of getting a degree. I didn't know at the time, but if I had taken business as a major I would have enjoyed it, and it would have been just what I needed.

Outside of the university, having nothing else lined up for a job, I accepted a position with Missoula Mercantile, where I had worked before the war for several years in various service jobs, as a janitor and night watchman while I was a student. The position was in the plumbing wholesale department. The goal was to be an outside salesman for the area. Although I had worked there before, I didn't have any training in the profession of plumbing. While there I learned some of the basics of the plumbing business, but I was not a happy warrior, partly because I wanted to control my own destiny.

One option I could have pursued would have been to become an airline pilot. I had pretty good credentials, about 950 hours (mostly B-24) of four-engine flying time, including some 'hairy' actual instrument time. A lot of us pilots had already qualified for a commercial pilot license, and I also had some leadership experience under pressure and two years of college from 1940-1942 as of January 1st, 1946. I also had no criminal record or DUI, to date anyway. This sounded pretty good for a change, but the trouble is I probably would have had to move to a big city like Chicago or Denver, even though the perks were good. Of course there were thousands of pilots leaving the service at this time and many had more flying time and experience than I had. And, finally, most would start out as copilots and might stay in that slot for some time. All in all I decided not to go for this route.

Another poor decision I made upon returning home was ordering a new Ford convertible. My dad was still working at Ford at the time. I didn't have a car during the war as I tried to economize, but the convertible wasn't too practical, and more expensive. I thought I deserved to have that, but it was foolish because it took a long time before they got a convertible in. Dad tried to talk me into getting a four-door or a sedan instead, a good used car should have been ok, but no, I wanted a convertible.

Although I made some mistakes upon my return to Missoula, after meeting Shirley Lee things really turned around. When I first saw her at a New Year's Eve party in 1946 I thought to myself, who's this little sweetie here! She just looked so cool, and she wore these cute little saddle shoes. Shirley was sitting on a sofa with her good friend Helen, from Roundup, Montana, who was about a year older. They were best friends when she had lived there. I made a date with her that evening and my initial impression proved to be right on! Shirley and I were married on June 25th, 1948.

Soon after we built a home in Orchard Homes, where my mom had bought five acres near South 3rd Street. My stepfather, Shirley's stepdad C.B., built it for us. I picked out a nice design, though perhaps my ideas were too big, and C.B. built most of it. He said he wanted to do something for me because I had served in the war. When I worked with C.B. on the house, I knew a little bit of plumbing, as I was supposed to be in training to be

Shirley and me

a wholesale plumbing salesman at Missoula Mercantile. I really didn't get far enough along in the training, but I did learn some and I helped C.B. do our plumbing, including work with soil pipe. It was educational.

Shirley with my parents on a picnic at Skalkaho Falls

I also tried to move my dog Shep to live with me and Shirley in Orchard homes. However, he didn't feel quite at home there. When we had first gotten married, Sara Jane Savage had given Shirley a white kitten for her birthday. We called it Kitty-Perk. It just purred really loud like a coffee percolator when you held it or had it in your lap. Shep knew he couldn't run it off or anything because he knew we liked it I guess, but when we'd go to work he would leave the house and return to Blaine Street, where my parents lived. It was a few years later, however, that good ol Shep was having too much trouble getting up out of his bed, and I decided to have him put down. He died in my arms at the ripe age of sixteen. Shep had been such a good dog and had given me companionship and pleasure.

With my Captain's bars - 1946
Taken by my friend Clark MacDonald

I got a Bachelor of Arts in history in 1948, but I did not want to be a history teacher. I'd taken science courses, but history was the one I could graduate in, the quickest one. I did absorb some information, by osmosis if nothing else, just by being exposed. The government also likes to see a degree, as does the air force reserves, which I later joined with Ken Marshall, the guy from Pony, Montana, so that was a benefit. I did get my promotion to captain and although most of my reserve time was not on pay status, it did qualify for a modest retirement starting at the age of 60 if I met the requirements. It was one of the smarter things I accomplished and I was also able to make some new friends through the reserves.

I also met people through my work at the Merc. It was interesting to get to know people in different trades, and I met a young man who was in the Culligan water conditioning business out of Hamilton. His name was 'Cap' Kramis and he had been a fighter pilot fighting with the British along with a few other Americans defending England. They came close to being overwhelmed by the Germans, but held on to victory. Before long he told me that he was going to sell his half of the business, and there would be a spot available to join with his partner. Shirley and I hadn't been married too long then, and I had been working at the Mercantile for about two years when I got the brainstorm that I wanted to buy into that business with Culligan soft water. We had already been more oriented towards Culligan and soft water because I had been raised on Blaine Street, which used the water supply from the Rattlesnake Creek and was relatively soft. I was also so wanting to get on my own and to be in my own business, so I took the offer. My partner was an older man about 70 or so by the name of Floyd Straighton. He was pleasant enough, but we had nothing in common. He was the brains of the outfit, you might say. I didn't know anything about business, but he was cordial to me and was a good salesman and had started the business from scratch. The water in Hamilton comes from wells and the water is hard, so when Floyd retired from the insurance business in Great Falls he had seen an opportunity for a franchise in the soft water business.

Since the job was in Hamilton we decided to sell our house in Missoula, the house that C.B. had done so much work on. We paid C.B., though not nearly as much as he deserved, but he had no hard feelings. The Culligan office was in Hamilton, so on May 1st, 1950 we moved up there for a five year stay, but we hadn't sold our house yet. Shirl was quite disturbed that I would turn around so soon after the house was built and sell it in order to get in the business, but I was under pressure to sell the house because I had committed to the local Culligan co-owner. It was a risky move doing that, but I was pretty bull-headed and I wanted to get out of the Merc. It was partly my ego, but I didn't want to be a clerk, which I basically had been up to that point, and I thought I should do better, but I didn't equip myself very well. Unfortunately that's the way life is sometimes, I didn't know business would interest me until it was right in front of me.

Shirl was working at the Bureau of Public Roads in Missoula at the time and it paid a pretty good salary. She was fortunate to be able to transfer to another federal job at Hamilton's Rocky Mountain Laboratory. At the time the lab's focus was research of Rocky Mountain spotted fever and the development of a preventative vaccine. Shirley got the job, the house eventually sold, the move was final, and we even had a baby on the way.

When we moved to Hamilton I became active in Post #47 of the American Legion.

I wanted to get acquainted with people when I could, and I was elected Post Commander after a period of time. In September of 1952 I attended a district Legion meeting in Paradise, Montana. I returned on a sunny Sunday afternoon when Shirl shocked me and said she might be coming down with polio. She was a realist, and said she had a terrific headache, which she practically never had, and was losing some strength in her arms. She was given a spinal tap at Daly Memorial Hospital the next morning confirming this. We were devastated and she was taken to St. Patrick's Hospital in Missoula by ambulance and I drove our car there. She was immediately put in isolation and I was only able to talk to her at the doorway of her room. All of us felt helpless and she was so worried about how our first baby would be, as he was due to be born in about a month. She went through a grim month of paralysis and worry, but Billy was quite healthy when he was born. It was a tremendous relief.

We named Bill after my brother, though William was also a tradition in the family, as it was my father's name as well. Dad was quite ill at the time of Billy's birth and died a few weeks afterwards. He knew that Bill had been born, however, and smiled at the news, but he was fading and the carbon monoxide poisoning from his work got to him in the end. He was 65 years old.

The way we lived our lives from then on was changed by Shirl's polio. Thankfully she had tremendous desire to recover as best as possible and take care of Billy and support me as well in my business later on.

I was in the Culligan water conditioning business for 23 years. The business was originally built on delivering soft water tanks to individual businesses or homes, and typically they would be changed every 28 days or more often depending on demand or needs. We had a driver and initially I'd go on the routes with him to learn the location of our tanks. These tanks weighed about 160 pounds. Most all of the tanks were located in a basement down a flight of steps, and with the weight of the cart and the tanks you were talking about 188 pounds. I wasn't too big and was in fair condition, but it was quite a chore for me to try to do a day's exchange work by myself if the driver was sick or if the route was longer than usual. Floyd and I alternated time monthly at the shop and regenerating tanks, but Floyd was too old to do any heavy lifting on the routes, so I'd be on the truck helping the driver or installing. So in theory I was a businessman, a route man, and a plumber installing units. Supposedly I was to help with selling too, but I was not very successful, I wasn't a salesman like Floyd had been in the past. This was a handicap because sales were essential for success and income. Floyd and his wife Leona (a retired nurse) were good to me and after Shirl got polio they would have me over at their home for meals fairly often when I was working up in Hamilton to help support us. I really appreciated her delicious meals.

We had a ten-year lease with the owner of the building with modest rent. It was quite a compact place. There was just room to backwash and regenerate the tanks and to back the truck in that carried the tanks in the evening. It was heated by one stove in the corner of the shop.

After about three years working with Floyd he sold his half interest to me and I became the sole owner. When I took over there were about two years left on the lease and the handwriting was on the wall that Missoula County had the potential to be the best market, as opposed to Hamilton and Ravalli County, so we made plans to eventually move the company down there.

We decided to move our residence to Missoula because Shirl was pregnant with our second child and she needed our family support. Billy had gotten to be a good little helper for her and he was four years old at that time. We didn't find a house that suited us or had a low down payment for about three months, so during that time we lived with my mother. We eventually found and bought a small two-bedroom house on the south outskirts of town and moved in on a bitterly cold November day in 1955. Our daughter Bette Lee was born nearly half a year later in April 1956.

When we moved back to Missoula I was still a member of the Missoula Air Reserve Squadron. People in the Hamilton area had appreciated the activation of their own squad shortly after I moved there in 1950. This made it easy to attend weekly meetings. As in Missoula, it was only classroom training and on a non-pay status, but it did allow us to stay active in the reserve.

The Missoula Squadron – me basking in the spotlight

When the lease expired in 1957 we also moved the operation down to Missoula to a small building on West Broadway, owned by Shirley's mother. It had served as a former location for her uncle's fuel oil business, so it had to be remodeled considerably a few weeks before our actual move to take care of our special needs.

Running the Culligan business was demanding, but I enjoyed contact with the customers. Most folks were very pleasant to deal with, and there emerged a feeling of loyalty between myself and my customers. As such, I wanted to give them the best service possible. However, as time went on, the competition became more active and began promoting home ownership and the use of automatic units. These units would regenerate on a time clock basis and could handle a lot more volume of water with no need to have somebody come by regularly like in our Culligan business. In a way we were like a juicy plum waiting to be picked by the competition because we had already installed the tanks. All the competition had to do was switch to their unit.

We sold automatic softeners as well, but what our business really needed was a good sales force, and I was never able to achieve that. I always valued our customers and did the best I could to provide good service and be a good employer to my employees. So when the competition came in with sharp high-pressure salesmen, it was very hard for me to accept customers saying they had switched to the competitor's automatic softener. Because of this sense of loyalty, it was a very tough on me. I thought I owned the customers since I had the feeling that I had treated them right, but that's not reality and I had to accept that and realize that's just the way business works, but it depressed me.

However, we did have some loyal customers and as one told me when she was approached by the competition, "I don't care what you have, I'VE GOT SERVICE!"

In another instance a local banker told me he talked to a man who had started a competitive soft water company in Missoula. When the banker asked what the hardest part of getting started in Missoula was, the man said it was the loyalty of customers to Bob Schottelkorb. So while I was moaning and groaning that was a testimonial and quite nice to know.

I did have some good employees through the years. After Floyd left I needed another person to help in the regeneration of tanks and to help the driver, so I hired a Hamilton senior high school student, Gordon Laridon, part-time at first. This proved to be a very good move because he was a hard and willing worker, and we got to be good friends even to this day. When I moved the operation to Missoula he actually moved down and worked with us until he was drafted into the army. Our faithful hardworking driver exchange-man of Hamilton drove to Missoula and helped us get the shop remodeled and in operation. He had a real work ethic, his name was Verdon France. We were fortunate to have had him. After we were settled in, he returned to Hamilton and other jobs. We also had a personable driver who was a good worker by the name of Cliff Iverson. He was with us for several years. We all got along well together, but he finally left for the U.S. Post Office and its great retirement benefits.

Cliff Iverson and Gordon Laridon: 1956

My mom died in 1960 just before our youngest, Bobbi Ann, was born (another October baby), and Mom left me some additional property on South 3rd Street West. I built a new Culligan facility that was fashioned with the needs of the business in mind, so that was a big change for the better. We had much improved facilities and a room to receive the salt truck, so when it came with the bulk deliveries it was much easier to handle.

Shirley tried to help out as well working part-time. At first she started out at home, then worked half-days when Bobbi Ann started Kindergarten. She was comfortable working in the office, as she didn't want people watching her, but I should have turned all of the bookwork over to her. For instance, if I had a bill I wanted to send out to somebody, sometimes I was a little bit resistant to charge what it required. Shirley was not that way, though, and she did what was needed in a prompt and efficient manner.

I still loved the outdoors like I had growing up, and in my spare time I continued to hunt and hike around beautiful Montana. In September 1959 I thought it would be neat to climb the Summit of Lolo Peak at 9,096 feet, which was a prominent landmark about fifteen to twenty miles south of Missoula. The road was steep in places and we had to navigate between large boulders because the road had been washed out by spring floods. I had taken my son Billy with me, as he was my buddy, and I didn't know if we were going to make it or not. Billy was a month shy of his seventh birthday, October 28th. I probably expected too much of him, the poor kid, but he didn't complain. The trail was fairly steep and we took brief rests, but Billy started to cry after climbing up quite a ways. We stopped, rested, and I talked to him, and then he said he thought he could continue. After we hiked a while it appeared we had reached the false summit. Bummer. We had our lunch and continued on, however, finally reaching our goal. What a beautiful view in all directions! I fired my rifle into the middle of the lake far below us and to my surprise I didn't see the ripple from the bullet until a few moments later because it was so far down. Of course, the Winchester 30-carbine didn't have a high velocity and it was a long ways down there. The trip back was much easier and rather uneventful. I was glad to make the hike and was very proud of Billy.

Hiking continued to be a tradition in my family. Fast-forwarding a generation, in September 1988, Bill, Bette and I took a hike along with Bill's young son Andy on the Highline Trail in Glacier National Park. The trail leads to Granite Park Chalet and eventually loops down to the parking lot, a considerable distance lower on the mountain. Andy was eight years old. We had hiked some distance and I was getting a little worried about him, as Andy started complaining his side hurt and he was tired. We stopped and rested for a while and Bill talked to Andy, just as I had talked to him when he had been young during our hikes. As we moved on, Bill continued a running conversation with Andy, which seemed to help. We had our lunch and some liquid refreshments at the chalet, and then hiked down through considerable undergrowth along the trail. We watched for a possible encounter with a grizzly bear, which inhabited the area. Bill and I each carried a can of bear spray with us, though thankfully we didn't need to use it. When we left the park, we had a nice supper in Coram at a restaurant which was very enjoyable being together as a family. History does repeat itself with young hikers and their dads.

In the early 1960s I did something that really broadened my horizons. I joined the Wilderness Society as well as the Montana Chapter. In the late spring the Montana Chapter would publish in the local paper a list of upcoming hikes in the area and these were free to sign up, typically with about ten to fifteen hikers. Bill and I and occasionally Bette took a few hikes, but with his busier high school life Bill no longer accompanied me when I started to take a few four-day horseback trips into the Bob Marshall wilderness area. For me, at least, on horseback was the only way I could attempt the distances involved and back while packing bedding and supplies.

Ever since I had heard about the Chinese Wall in the Bob Marshall Wilderness I wanted to go there and see it. It was a remarkable rock formation. It runs north and south for several miles as part of the Continental Divide. The western slope is more like a typical mountain, but the east side is mostly sheer cliffs of several hundred feet high. Horseback is the way most people would experience it, but a few rugged hikers could do the same. It was Elizabeth Hannum, a remarkable middle-aged woman, who was able to convince some outfitters to sponsor low cost four-day trips. Upon checking the Internet for Liz's background for this book, I was startled to discover her name was Elizabeth Reitell-Smith. I'm guessing she was still using her previous name for a short period, but at any rate she was one in the same person. After her move to Missoula, she became the publication director for the University of Montana school of Forestry. She also worked as a director of the Montana Wilderness Society for thirteen years and continued to be an environmental advocate for the rest of her life. Liz was from New York City, but after a trip into 'the Bob' she was hooked and moved to Missoula, Montana. Fortunately she wanted to share the wilderness experience with others. The society was happy to have her on board to lead the way. The Outfitters charged 30 dollars a day and furnished the horses, tents, food, and cooked the hearty meals. We guests only had to furnish our own bedroll and personal gear. What a bargain!

Aerial view of the magnificent Chinese Wall, taken after the trip

My first trip with the Wilderness Ride was with Tom Edwards, who had a ranch along the north fork of the Blackfoot River near the wilderness. There were about ten or twelve of us including Liz. The first day was a fairly easy one as we didn't have too far to travel for our first overnight stay. I had very little experience with horses, so that was fine with me. If we needed a break we were able to walk for a while, leading the horse, to relieve and ease some of our stiffness. The Outfitter tried to match temperament of the horses to the experience of the dudes, so mine was quite a mild horse. At one stop we were able to see the impressive roaring river at a very narrow stretch through rocky cliffs. We could hear it as we approached, but couldn't see it very readily because the river was about 80 feet below ground level. We dismounted and crawled along the ground to peer over the rim to see it.

We spent the night at the north fork cabin owned by the Forest Service. Most of us rolled out our bedrolls on the floor and the wood stove served us supper and breakfast. We voted on where we would go the next day, deciding to see the triple divide. From the top of this point any water flowed either to the Pacific, the Atlantic, or into Hudson Bay in Canada. From there we continued to Danaher Basin where some hearty souls in the late 1860s had attempted to grow wild hay there and make a go of it. A few rusted implements were all that remained. The season apparently was just too short and the weather too rugged to be practical. We continued our loop of the area and back to the ranch on the fourth day.

In June of 1965 I made my second trip to the Bob Marshall. I remember the date because it was the summer after severe flooding in the spring of 1964. The conditions were this: an above-average snow pack in Glacier National Park, and unusually warm spring rains on both sides of the Continental Divide. I'm sure the outfitters couldn't host any dudes for several months in the summer of '64. Besides swamping their ranches, it also took out roads and trails. I had chosen a trip with Ken Gleasen, a rancher who was on the east side of the divide along the Teton River. Signs of devastation were still visible from the previous year, where several log cabins and a barn had been hit hard, but they had cleared out most of the debris and were back in business. I took to Ken and his family right away, including his young son, Joe, who was in his early twenties. Everyone was very friendly and Ken knew his backpacking trade very well. Liz Hannum was along, as well as George Weisel, a botany professor at the University of Montana. There were about the usual mix of dudes in the group, and while Liz and George were guests they were pros when it came to helping out with Ken's crew when needed.

Again the temperament of horses was matched with the experience of the riders. My assigned horse was named Peanuts and he and I weren't too remarkable. He was ok until I wanted to pause and take a picture, but he was afraid of being left behind so I had trouble getting him to wait. Afterwards he would hurry to catch up with the others, poor baby.

With Peanuts

This was the trip when I got to see the Chinese Wall close up. I can't remember if it took more than one day or not, but usually we traveled about eighteen to twenty-two miles a day. At any rate, it was pretty tiring for me and it was great to camp near the wall. Ken used tipi-type tents for the guests and I had a small one for myself. It was adequate, and I could stand upright in it instead of being hunched over.

After the tiring ride I was quite stiff, so I decided to sit by the rushing stream to take a nice drink of the cold water. George Weisel soon walked up with a small flask of whiskey. He poured out a little into my cup and I took it willingly.

We chatted for a bit, then he repeated the favor. I soon realized that these two shots were just what the doctor ordered and my pain and stiffness were gone. I was pleasantly surprised. No doubt it didn't hurt my ability to carry on the conversation either, but it was just the right solution for my bod.

The next morning I was still sleeping when Liz called out, "You'd better get up Bob while the sun is still shinning on the wall!"

So I hurriedly dressed and indeed it was a beautiful sight. The sun illuminated the incredible rock wall formation, making it even grander.

Breakfast was delicious as usual and I felt very content as we started on the trail again. Sometimes I rode near Liz and George and they would enlighten me on the names of the wildflowers and other things of nature. I enjoyed the presence of Liz and the professor, but on the fourth day we headed back to the ranch, signaling the end of our journey, though I vowed to come again.

On the trail in the Bob

The next year I enjoyed my second four-day ride with Ken, Joe, Liz, and George, so we all got a little better acquainted with each other and the crew. This time it was a trip to the northern extension of the wall. The snow hadn't completely disappeared and once, when riding along the trail, one of the pack mules slipped down the hillside about twenty feet or better. There was no panic and the rest of the pack string waited for the crew to rescue their trail mate. Ken handed me the reins of the string of mules while he and Joe went down to unload the heavy burden off the mule and help it back on the trail. I didn't have any experience with handling mules and I spoke loudly to my mule to show I was in charge and in control. It probably wondered why this dude was raising his voice to tell it to stay calm. No doubt I was the one needing to stay calm. I was glad to turn the reigns back to Ken, and we were on our way again.

George in the back row third from left, me and Liz in the front row on the left

Later on we got to go into the high country along the Continental Divide and I enjoyed the vast expanse of the wilderness and the variety of wildlife. It was a pleasure to see and hear the sharp whistle of the hoary marmot, which eerily broke the silence. The hoary marmot was a fair size and when it stood up to proclaim its presence I could see that its upper body was silver colored, but its lower body appeared to be plain brown or rust colored. To me it looked as if the marmot had put on a clean white shirt, but stayed in its scrubby work pants.

Then the tiny pica would let you come quite close as it scurried among the rocks. It knew it had to stay busy cutting the grass with its teeth with the grass growing in small patches in open areas. After the grass dried they would store it undercover for a long winter ahead, just like a squirrel does with seeds and nuts. This was my last trip to the Bob, other events seemed to get my attention as time went on, but I will always remember these trips with pleasure and be thankful these wilderness areas exist.

I also continued to take quite a few hikes with my son Bill throughout the years. The one we took in August 1967 was pretty neat. Our goal was to cross the Mission Mountain Range starting in the Swan Valley north of the Condon Ranger Station and then head west to come out at Eagle Pass, east of Allen Town on Highway 93. This did not require mountain climbing skills or super endurance, just a desire to explore a beautiful area. Bill had just graduated from the eighth grade, was close to fifteen years old, and also had just become an eagle scout. Shirley, Bette, and Bobbi Ann accompanied us as we drove approximately 85 miles to the turn off to an old logging road that was pretty level, but I missed the trailhead sign. We drove until the road ended and instead of turning back to locate the trailhead, which would have been the smart thing, Bill and I just took off uphill and cut across the steep hillside. The area had also just finished some August showers that had lasted a week or so, and we were soon wet clear through. Basically we did it the hard way. We didn't even stop at the ranger station for help and didn't have too accurate a map. I also should have notified them of Shirl's location since she was several miles on the back road, and if she had had any car trouble no one would have known.

We didn't meet any other hikers on the trail we had found, so we were alone in this beautiful forest, and we made it to our first camp just beyond Hemlock Lake. After the first night we followed a good trail heading west up a fairly steep mountain, but the trail suddenly ended after we got up a ways. I looked again at the map and it showed that we should just keep going on the trail, so I determined that what we were on wasn't a trail at all, not a Forest Service trail at least. Not sure what else to do, we just kept heading northwest in the general direction we knew we should go, and that evening we camped by a small, you might say a pothole, lake. As we ate supper, a lone mountain goat appeared on a rocky point above us a relatively short distance away. The sun was still shining on him while we were in the shade. He really looked majestic. Standing on a high point on a rock, he would look to the west for several minutes, then turn around and do the same thing in the other direction, just like he was enjoying the view. This went on for about 45 minutes and it was very peaceful and enjoyable. As night fell things got less peaceful, and at one point I heard Bill shouting and yelling. I jumped up and grabbed my 357 revolver, expecting a bear, but it turned out he was just having a nightmare. We didn't see anything other than a few deer on our trip. Bear spray hadn't been discovered at that time, but I sure would have carried it.

The next day we headed down toward Summit Lake, our next goal, and refilled our water supply. It was a bright sunny day when we started climbing the east side of Eagle Pass. The hillside was pretty steep, but was covered with beautiful bright flowers. Dozens of hummingbirds were at work on the flowers and were hovering all around us as we hiked upward. The day continued to get warm, and our water supplies were starting to run low enough for me to start getting concerned. However, as luck would have it, after seeing no one else for days, we met a pack string with horses and mules coming down toward us on the good zig-zag trail. The guide introduced himself and asked if we needed water. So that was a blessing and we gulped down some water and refilled our canteens. I asked the guide about the trail we had been on disappearing. He said that wasn't a Forest Service trail but an old Indian trail forbidden to outsiders, as they didn't want others to know where they liked to hunt. After our brief exchange with the guide, we made sure that they knew we appreciated their help and continued on our way. We were getting tired and hot when we finally reached the pass. Soon we reached a cool ravine, shaded by large cedar trees and complete with ferns and running water. From there it was all downhill and easy hiking, especially since we were now on the actual trail.

Well, it was mission accomplished, and dear Shirl and the girls had recently parked where we planned to meet them. Bobbi, our youngest, was bitten by a horse fly just after we got there, so that kind of spoiled her part of the reunion, but it was nice having the whole family together again.

The Missions are a beautiful mountain range, and Bill and I occasionally went back there, sometimes just the two of us but other times we went in groups with people from the Wilderness Society. Our hike to Cliff Lake was led by a 60-year-old forest service employee. At the start of the hike he didn't seem to know just where the trailhead was, so he just started bushwhacking through the woods, setting a fast pace. I was usually at the back and before I knew it I was lost. Bill was with me, but I was pretty put out that he didn't make any effort to see if we were all there. So after some frustrating yelling we connected again and I think he slowed up a little. It was getting toward noon when we stopped for lunch and here our leader redeemed himself in my eyes when he got out a pretty big kettle and he started making some soup for everyone. That really hit the spot. I had my own lunch, but that was a plus. After that I perked up more and was able to keep up, and we also finally hit a trail that was headed up toward the lake, so things looked a lot brighter and I started visiting with some of the other hikers.

When we got to Cliff Lake to camp for the night there wasn't much room along the sloping shore to pitch your tent. Bill and I shared a small tent. We got a fire going for us and I boiled some water. I put a beef bouillon cube in his cup and when that dissolved it made a salty soup. He loved that. It was an unexpected treat.

At the camp that night a lone airman met up with us and said he had met a grizzly with a cub. Apparently they had come running towards him on the trail. He carried a small folding shotgun and he had come close to shooting the grizzly, but something had changed his mind and by stepping off to the side the grizzly went right by him. The grizzly and the cub were just trying to escape him and he wanted to avoid them. We went to bed with that spooky story in mind, but woke up around midnight. Some members of the group were yelling about water and we realized that a brief cloud burst was occurring. Since it was such a small lake the water had risen and gotten into their tents. We were up a little higher, but soon we too felt water at the foot of our bed, and we had to get up and move to a large communal campfire.

A little sleep-deprived the next day, we headed back. Bill and I were with two or three other hikers and we came across a rocky mountainside. The other hikers started to climb up it and I grudgingly decided to do the same.

Finally I said to myself, "What in the world am I doing? I'm not enjoying this. I'm not a rock climber!" So I quit and Bill and I started going back down to the trailhead, but it wasn't long before I realized I'd left my camera back there, so I went back by myself and I hiked as fast as I could back and got it. I hustled since I wanted to regroup with the others as soon as possible and also didn't want to come across a bear. Thankfully I didn't encounter one, and I rejoined the group at a restaurant in one piece.

Another trip Bill and I took started at Fort Benton, a small pioneer town about 80 miles northeast of Great Falls, Montana. The town has quite a history, located on the Missouri River where the old-time steamboats had to unload their cargo and passengers since the Missouri River at Fort Benton could no longer be navigated further west because of the low water. The town itself is like a step back into time with old frontier-style buildings complete with a historical waterfront museum and lots of cottonwoods, which, in the early days, were fuel for the steamboats. The town was established in 1841 as a fur trading post by the American Fur Company, and they traded furs with the Blackfeet Indians.

Gordon Laridon accompanied Bill and I and Clark MacDonald, my friend from the

Mexico trip years earlier. To navigate the waters we brought our small fifteen-foot boat from Missoula. It wasn't too well suited for this trip because it didn't have an open bow, so that made it awkward to try to jump toward the riverbank when you wanted to stop along the way. It had a 35-horsepower mercury outboard motor and that tended to load up and foul the spark plugs when we were idling in the current, but that was all we had available for us. We were pretty well loaded as we had a tent, sleeping bags, the necessary food, water, and cooking gear. I also brought along a rubber raft about ten feet long and we towed that behind the boat and that would haul a lot of our camping gear.

One thing that was noticeably different in the environment here was the soil. Where west of the divide we had more sand and gravel along the river, here the runoff created thick, muddy water as the banks eroded away. It seemed to be a waste, but that was nature's way and was why we had a hard time avoiding mud each time we stopped. We didn't stop off to do some hiking along the way as we had a schedule to meet.

We were a little concerned when we passed Arrow Creek at the flood stage, as it was shooting directly into the Missouri as we passed by. The rubber raft bounced around quite a bit, but we continued onward. We were impressed by the white cliffs as we floated by, and they lined the north side of the river as we headed east. They were sandstone and weren't real high, but quite beautiful to behold with the different formations that Mother Nature had carved them into. Lewis and Clark had also been quite impressed with the cliffs on their trip up the Missouri in May of 1805. There were more individual spires and formations of different shapes that appeared from time to time as we continued our journey and floated through the area designated as a wild river preserve. This included Cow Island, where Chief Joseph had led his band of Nez Perce Indians across the river to escape the pursuing US Army. They had refused to be on a reservation and had hoped to reach Canada, but they were exhausted and short of food for the women and children and the elderly that were with the warriors. It was near here that the army caught up with them and they had to surrender.

We ended our three-day journey at Kip State Park, where the Fred Robinson

Highway Bridge crossed the river. It was 149 miles from our start in Fort Benton. Gordon and Clark stayed there while Bill and I caught a ride hitch-hiking back to Fort Benton. We didn't have to wait too long for a ride and at Fort Benton we got my pickup and returned to Clark and Gordon. We hooked up the boat and went back again to our starting point. There Clark left us and returned to his home and Gordon took the pickup with the boat back to Missoula.

Shirley met us in Fort Benton with our car and Bill and I joined Shirl and Bette and Bobbi for a trip to Billings, Montana. At Billings, Bill boarded a train to return to Missoula. He was going to take a driver's education class that was available before the start of his freshman year at Sentinel High School. We would miss him on our trip as a family, but his life was just opening up and it was a logical thing for him to do. Shirl and the girls and I continued with our pre-planned trip to the Black Hills of South Dakota to view the impressive Mt. Rushmore. With federal funding the work started in 1927 and finished in 1941, blasting and drilling the rock mountainside to carve the heads of the four presidents, Washington, Jefferson, Lincoln and Theodore Roosevelt out of solid stone. Impressive. The sculptures and Visitor's Center were separate from the Crazy Horse Memorial, which was started in 1948 and privately financed. Crazy Horse was a Lakota warrior chief who led his warriors against General George Armstrong Custer in the Battle of the Little Big Horn in his opposition to the settlers in the Dakotas. This huge memorial was in the area, but a different mountain, and was the dream of a Polish sculpture Korczak Zoilowski. Work on it continues to this day with his widow and several of their children among the workers on this nonprofit foundation. Seeing these two memorials was a worthwhile family trip and we returned to Missoula.

In 1961 during the Cold War with the Soviet Union the Air Force Reserve, which I had joined in 1945 and had now become squadron commander of a small unit, decided to use some of its reservists to man a new concept. The plan was to provide a place for the active duty air force units so that they could temporarily send some of their airplanes and crews to scattered civilian airports in the event of a possible soviet missile attack. Our squadron was under the 8638th Air Force Reserve Center in Spokane, Washington. In Missoula we were the 9604th Air Force Recovery squadron. Four other squadrons were assigned, two in Montana, in Helena and Billings, as well as one at Walla-Walla, Washington and Pendleton, Oregon. All five of us squadron commanders met for a meeting in Spokane and we met our group commander Colonel Charles Packard who was a teacher in civilian life at Washington State College in Cheney.

Without realizing it I led our squadron using the style of Major Fletcher, who had been our squadron commander at Fort Bliss Texas in the second and third phase of combat training. He would hold a critique after flying each mission in our B-24s. In our case here in Missoula we would have the session at the start of each training day to fill everybody in and let them provide some knowledge and a chance to participate in the planning of our goal to qualify for the plans laid out by the Air Force Reserve. At a later date Colonel Packard told me I was the only squadron commander of the five who he hadn't had complaints about. We were far from perfect, but that sounded pretty good to me. Another time a brigadier general who headed an inspection team from the region headquarters in California showed his appreciation as we were walking around outside of our headquarters. He put his arm around me and we walked a short distance. I didn't say anything and he didn't either, but I thought he was showing me his silent approval of us.

Well, my glory days in the reserves came to a sudden end in July 1964. About a month earlier the group had informed us that our active duty Staff Sergeant James Longacre, who had been our air force honcho from day one, was being reassigned and for us he would be hard to replace. He was quite the entrepreneur and really livened the place up. But the worst part was it appeared that he wasn't to be replaced at all. Maybe this was a way of admitting the air force was thinking about phasing out the reserve recovery program. At any rate, it was devastating to me, and the air force ended the recovery program within a few months. My morale was at a low point and I reluctantly resigned from my position as squadron commander. Colonel Packard and LT Col. Korsborn came over from Spokane and I was also honored by my squadron and by the headquarters in a brief retirement ceremony. As fate would have it, my promotion to Lieutenant Colonel came through shortly before this, and I was transferred to the inactive reserves.

In February of 1973 I left the Culligan business, which made losing the reserve force even harder. I wasn't able to sell for the price that I wanted, but I was happy that J.B. Yonce bought it. J.B. had been a very good exchange-man for me, so he knew the business. He was young, energetic, and a former marine. He hired his brother Steve to help out and it was good for the business because it brought in new vigor. J.B. was happy to have Shirley continue working in the office, as she had a good knowledge of the business and could answer questions as they arose. She was good with the customers as well. As the time passed J.B. sold the business to Tom Troxell and the workers continued to appreciate Shirley and her advice and counsel when they requested it.

I, however, was 'burnt out' and had been depressed at times, so I did have periods when I would return to the comfort of the outdoors and camp out with my pickup. It had a topper so I could drive out somewhere and sleep in relative comfort. I did some solo roaming of the Forest Service roads in western Montana and northern Idaho as well as going to Forest Service lookouts and old logging roads. When we first moved back to Missoula I used to hike in the O'Brien creek area south of Missoula where the mule deer were and enjoyed the scenery and the exercise. Fortunately I bought a small used Honda Trail 90 motorcycle during this period. It was quiet and relatively light with a simple design without the normal shift mechanism. If you needed to travel up a steep slope you had to stop and engage the stand and get off and move a lever to get into a low gear, so it was pretty cumbersome, but effective, and it allowed me to take some neat rides for miles on old roads and into Lolo Canyon to the south and elsewhere. Later on, if I wanted to stay two or three days, I would load it on my pickup's front bumper and this allowed me access further into the country and northern Idaho. This included areas where Lewis and Clark had headed west in 1805 and then when they returned the following year.

Exploring the Lewis and Clark Route

I still owned the Culligan building in 1973 and I had bought a small trailer court with a rental house on Catlin Street several years earlier. The trailer court really turned out to be a good investment and I enjoyed working there when I could, but it was a long-term investment with little cash income. After a few months I realized that I should look for a job, as we weren't too flush with money. I did register with the local employment service, but I found that the prospects for a middle-aged man who had been self-employed were not too great. I did, however, take a job as a custodian and night watchman for less than a year, but I began to feel I was sleeping my life away. Later I took a one year job as foreman with a small crew of the U.S. Forest Fire Lab helping on special work needs. It was nice to have a job with fair pay and no investment needed, but the program did end at one year.

Working at the fire lab, however, did get me in the mood to be active again, so that was good. After looking around for several months, I decided to buy a motel in February of 1978. It was a 22-unit motel in downtown Missoula. In a way it was like jumping from the frying pan into the fire, mostly because of the high price I paid.

Shirl had warned me, "If you buy that, it's your baby." Her mother had bought a four-unit motel after Shirl's dad had died and it really tied them down, but it had provided a place for them to live.

When I first took over the motel I didn't have anyone hired to be the resident operator, so that was me. I operated on adrenaline for the first two or three weeks, but this couldn't last. I was exhausted and didn't really know the business. I had some temporary managers for a while, though I finally lucked out and hired a great couple as live-in managers, Jim and Jennie Jones. They were just what the doctor ordered, as the saying goes. They were managers of another small hotel, but weren't happy with the owner's false promises. They moved in and took over along with their son Steve. There were two bedrooms and an area serving as kitchen and dining room, plus a small laundry area and office.

I would often have lunch with them and they treated me like family. I brought my own lunch, but sometimes Jim would cook up a pot of white beans and a good-sized ham and make corn bread, so that took precedence. Jennie was a great host and would greet people with a warm, friendly welcome. They were both friendly and outgoing as well as honest. We got along great. Jennie was good at supervising the maids, as she expected good housekeeping from them. The maids were a lot happier with our new management team. I relied on the Jones' years of experience and I paid as good a salary for them and the maids as I could, so that certainly helped.

I was happy to make improvements as often as I could as long as business was decent. The previous owner had been very frugal and tried to get by cheaply in all aspects of the business. One of the first improvements I made was to install central air conditioning in the office and living quarters. Jennie could not have survived without it.

One thing that worked out nicely was that our daughter Bette had just graduated from Eastern Montana College (now Montana State University Billings) in the spring with a degree in education as a special education teacher. This made her available to be a maid for the busy summer season. She was a good worker and pleasant, just as I expected. That fall she moved 120 miles north to Kalispell and became a teacher in the Evergreen School District. It was nice to have her help out early on and it worked out well for both of us. Later on, our younger daughter Bobbi Ann also worked as a maid for two summers and also did well. She graduated from Montana State University in Bozeman as a nurse.

Another maid we had was Lil. She was older and slower, and she loved to talk. She was friendly, but the other maids would tell me Lil is not keeping her end of the workload. So I tried to give her a pep talk without being nasty. Later she moved to Colorado to be near her daughter. She wrote me a little note and said that she really wanted to give me a hug when she left but she didn't know whether that would be proper.

Customers would also occasionally leave messages. Most were brief and to the point. "Nice place, nice price, nice to have a clock radio. Good showers, warm – thanks."

People from near and far stayed over, sometimes with interesting grammar: "Very comfortable bed. Sure slepted good. Nice and clean also. – North Dakotans."

Some notes were quite heartfelt: "We want to compliment you on a very nice motel room, fair, cleanliness, smelling fresh, a nice shower and accommodations, coffee, etc. It beats the Best Western all to heck. Plus the price is great. Glad we drove around last night and found you. We will recommend you to our family and friends. – Room 9 from Hillsboro, Oregon."

And others more personal: "Dear Folks, We've stayed in motels all across Canada and most of the USA, some were fancier some were newer, but none had the touch yours seems to have. 'Nice and homey' and clean. If you ever come to West VA, look me up – I cure awfully good ham and I'll serve you a meal."

All in all my time with the motel was a pleasant experience while the Jones were managers. I was able to draw a fair salary and generally enjoyed the experience. Problems would pop up from time to time, but we overcame them.

Jenny and Jim Jones with their son Steve and dog Nikki

In the summer of 1987 Jennie's health began to falter due to her heart problems. Although I would have liked to have continued on for a couple more years, I wouldn't do it without Jim and Jennie. It had been nine and a half years and I would be 65 in October. The new owner was anxious to move in during the remaining tourist season, so we closed a deal August 15th, 1987. It sold for considerably less than I had paid, but I had paid off about that amount anyway on my mortgage. I did manage to give Jim and Jennie a 2,500 dollar bonus, and if I could have managed it I would have doubled that. They weren't expecting anything, I don't believe, and they were really happy with the surprise. I continued to visit them after their retirement in their nice rented house on Plymouth Street. Jennie had several years to enjoy the home with Jim before she passed away. I certainly learned a lot from them and they were good to me.

By selling the motel and my little trailer court, I was able to stay connected with Mother Nature by buying an eight acre piece of land on Mt. Jumbo. I nicknamed it 'the ranch', but it didn't resemble a ranch in the slightest. There wasn't a lot of property, no running water, and of course I had no animals.

In the spring of 1992 I met my friend Jack G. Swartzman, a former logger who had moved to Missoula from Superior after his wife died of cancer. I really liked that he had been a logger and appreciated the outdoors and nature. Jack and I worked on 'the ranch' cutting brush and tree limbs that were low and I worried about lightning strikes and forest fires. He became my hunting partner too, so that worked out and we became good friends.

Although 'the ranch' wasn't too practical for me, it was a special place with many tall pine trees on its sloping hillside and I liked being close to town. On one cold March

Jack Schwartzman burning slash at 'the ranch'

day at the ranch Jack and I were sawing and cutting brush and tree limbs. It was lunch time and we were going to sit on the pickup tailgate. The air was chilly and there was a breeze blowing, so we got in the cab where it was warm with the sun from the east. Dusty Deschamps, the neighbor, had his sheep grazing not far from us and his llama as well, which was a guard for them. While we were eating we looked up at the sheep all moving downhill. The llama looked alarmed. Lo and behold right down the side of our property through the trees where it opened up a little were four bears. A black bear and three good-sized cubs in a tight group with one cub beside the mother and two close behind. They were loping in perfect stride and the sun glistened off their fur. It was a sight to behold, all taking place 150 feet or so in front of us. The sheep were naturally startled by them, and the gap was beginning to close between them. I got so excited I laid on the horn. I was afraid the bears were going to go over there and massacre them! The bears got frightened then and kept going on down the hill and made a sweep around and out of sight and presumably turned and ran up on the hill where it was less populated. Their coordination and agility was just like a drill team, it was amazing. Another time we were working and something made us look up. Here were three great grey owls gliding by and they landed on top of the tall pine trees nearby. They lingered a little while and came back the next day as well. It was beautiful. 'The ranch' was a neat place that way.

I'd bought 'the ranch' in October '84. Just days later, while boating on Flathead Lake, we spotted a 'for sale' sign on a cabin, owned by Dean and Harold Greiner from Polson. I had met Dean coming back from Boston at the end of the war. Previously our family and I had rented a cabin each year for a week or two on the lake at Pine Glen, which was nearby. This property had this little dock going out and nobody was there when we pulled up. All of us got out on the dock and the neighbor came out and wanted to know what we were doing, so we introduced ourselves and were soon hooked on the cabin. Shirl was worried we would never get it since I had just bought 'the ranch'. However, I had just sold my little trailer court, and my daughter Bette agreed to buy a minor interest in the property since she had a steady income as a teacher. All of that along with some hard bargaining, and the bank and the owner gave the sale the green light to go ahead. It was kind of risky at first, but it eventually proved to be a wise choice. Shirl loved the water and could go to the lake on the weekends, or when I was off on my hiking adventures.

Shirley at the lake cabin on Flathead Lake, just as it was when we bought it

As I have mentioned, most of my hikes were with Bill, as he was four years older than Bette and eight years older than our youngest Bobbi Ann. But in August of 1983 our two girls, who were now in their twenties, and I took a five day hike in the Bitterroot Selway Wilderness. We took my pickup and drove to the trailhead at Hoodoo Lake in northern Idaho. We were accompanied by my good friend Gordon Laridon, his wife Donna, and their daughter Kelley, who all dropped us off after we shared a late lunch and drove the pickup back to town. Our plan was to fly out on the fifth day, as Gordon had made arrangements for us to be picked up.

Our packs were pretty heavy, mine was about 40 pounds and the girls' nearly as much, but we had a nice adventure and beautiful scenery. After hiking to the higher ridge, we camped there for the first night, enjoying plump huckleberries along the way. The next day we dropped down to the east fork of Moose Creek where there were lots of cedar trees and large ferns wet from rain. We got wet feet, and our wet shoes made it tough on our feet so we had to use tape and band aids to try to avoid blisters. Dry socks were at a premium.

Gordon and Donna Laridon at an air show

Blisters avoided for the most part, we reached the Moose Creek Ranger Station on the third day, where the small airstrip was located. There were a few improved camping spots around the airstrip and we noticed signs that said to beware of rattlesnakes and not to shoot them, but to notify the station when they were spotted.

We were walking down a trail single file with me in the lead when Bette yelled, "There's a snake right by the trail where you passed, Dad!"

I looked where Bette was pointing and sure enough, there was the rattlesnake. I threw a pine cone at it from a respectable distance and it moved away from the area. After that we got a little leery and were more careful.

Hot and weary from our travels, we were looking for the camping spot near the airstrip which the personnel at the ranger station told us about. When we finally found it, we were disappointed because there were a lot of flies and yellow jackets zooming around. So we continued a little ways down the mighty Selway, a beautiful unspoiled river, and found a place to camp just a short distance away, leaving most of the nuisance insects behind. We really enjoyed swimming here just as we had done along the east fork.

On the fourth day we headed back to camp near the airstrip. We had promised we would be at the strip at 8am the next day for pickup. After a rather slim breakfast, since we were almost out of our food, we scanned the rainy and cloudy sky and listened for our airplane. It was a relief when Tom Oertli of Hamilton landed his Cessna 180. After greetings, Tom loaded us up and we were on our way. We climbed steadily in the smooth air and marveled how the landscape passed by quickly below us. We leveled off at 7300 feet heading east and Tom pointed out landmarks along the way as we flew over to Bear

Bobbi and Bette with our pilot Tom Oertli

Creek Canyon coming out at Lost Horse Pass and down into the Bitterroot Valley below. The mountains passed quickly from view as we descended and Lake Como soon appeared off to the right. I was impressed by how everything seemed so green. After about a half hour flight, we landed at the Hamilton airport. Our car was parked right next to Tom's hanger right where Gordon had left it as previously arranged. How nice, thanks Gord. It was a good adventure for us, only next time I wouldn't mind having a little pack animal to haul our gear.

In 1987 I'd read about the Grand Canyon in the National Geographic Traveler. It had a detailed article and great photos telling about the hikes, the beauty, and what it took to hike the canyon. So that fall, with my little Toyota Camry hatchback I decided to make a trip to see for myself how I could arrange a trip with Bill and Bette in the spring of 1988. I had removed the backseat of the car and made it so I could sleep there with my feet sticking into the trunk area. Shirl fixed some towels covering the windows so it gave me some privacy and all in all, enabled me to travel economically.

The Grand Canyon is a very busy place. People are constantly coming and going up and down the trail, but it is remarkable the views you get. On the south rim it's pretty civilized and there's not much in the boonies, but on the north rim there are areas outside the park where you can camp. I stopped at the north rim and decided to hike down the trail leading to the Roaring Springs, where a huge amount of water gushes out from the side of the canyon. It was a pleasant hike down and I had my lunch there, as I had packed sandwiches. I didn't want to linger too long because the day was warming up and I had the five-mile hike back up to the rim. Fortunately I was traveling light. After my little hike I inquired at the tourist information center about how to obtain a permit, as you had to arrange a reservation nearly a year ahead of time. But I was able to make a reservation for Bette, Bill and I to stay two nights at the Phantom Ranch on the campgrounds on the north side of the Colorado River. It coincided with Bette's spring break, around April.

So the following spring, Bill, Bette and I left Missoula. I took my four wheel drive pickup thinking that if we were to drive off the paved road in some area with loose sand we

Bill, Bette, and me on the North Rim

would be able to get out. This vehicle wasn't too comfortable, however, and poor Bette was crowded in the middle most of the way, but she didn't complain. I had arranged for us to hike down the South Kaibab Trail on the south rim. The first night we stayed at a cabin on the south rim, and the next morning we took a bus to the Kaibab trail. It is a shorter hike, the shortest route to take to the Phantom Ranch, but it is steeper and about nine miles to the ranch. Everything was new to us, so we were quite impressed by the steep trail and the view of the various areas that opened up to us as we progressed down the steep grade. Occasionally we would encounter a mule train going down to the canyon carrying tourists, but some of the trails looked pretty spooky to be high up on the back of a mule. However, they are very well trained and it's an old trick to them, but I still wouldn't do it.

At the Phantom Ranch the sleeping accommodations were two small dormitories for about twenty people, the women in one dorm, the men in another. They held about ten bunk beds with bathroom facilities. Bill and I were in with several different groups of men that were all very friendly and enjoying their own adventures. We were pretty weary and happy that we had made it and it was quite warm. The next day we rested and relaxed more and only explored the immediate area.

On the third day we had an early breakfast at the dining room and got underway heading a little further south to go across the Silver Bridge, a utility bridge that carried the water from the Roaring Springs in a large pipe slung underneath the bridge. This trail, the Bright Angel Trail, was about twelve miles long and wasn't quite as steep and had a few places where you could get water. It also wasn't used by the mules and was more scenic and had more green vegetation than the barren area of the South Kaibab Trail. We'd had about all we could handle on the hike, but by sticking to our schedule we were determined to successfully complete it even though we were getting quite weary. Each mile-marker was a relief and required a mini celebration to keep us going. When we finally made it up to the top there was a bench that we gratefully collapsed onto.

That was all right for a nice break, but when we tried to get up, our muscles had set and we could barely walk. It was like we were suddenly old people, (I speak from experience now). We had reserved a room for that evening on the south rim and we also wanted to go to the nearby town, Tusayan, just outside of the park. Finally at our destination, the first thing we did was call Shirl at home and tell her we had made it. Bette made the call and before handing it over to me, Bill said, "Tell her the colonel would like to talk with her." That really cracked us up, as Shirl was not taken in by military brass. After we finished our phone call, it was time for dinner, which was a relief after such a long hike. We really appreciated that meal and our sense of accomplishment.

Then we decided we would go to an IMAX theater. I had never been to one before. And what do they do, they have a huge screen displaying the video and it's as if you were in a helicopter. Zooming toward cliffs, it got me all shook up.

I kept wanting to say, "Pull up! Pull up!" and Bette got quite a kick out of me gripping the armrests and trying to fly. But it was all because it was just like I was flying, and I had to eventually close my eyes because it was too realistic. It was quite an experience.

When we went back to the park and to our room I thought it would be good to order a hot buttered rum for all of us, but I found out everything was closed up for the night. It was only about 9 o'clock, but with all these weary hikers things close down early. So we had to forego that.

On the way back home we made our trip back along the north rim for a ways, then into Utah and up north back to Montana. All in all we felt that we had accomplished something, and I had arranged for two of our three kids to see the canyon, which had gotten to be a goal of mine. I paid for as much as I could of the expenses because I knew that Bill and Bette were on a tight budget as much as I was. But I wanted to make it possible for them.

In 1991, three years later, I arranged for a more inclusive family trip that would start at the north rim and again hike down to the Phantom Ranch, and then back up the Bright Angel Trail on the south rim. This included Bill and Bette, as before, but also Bobbi and her husband John Combs, as well as Bill's son Andy, who was now eleven, and Bill's father-in-law Ivan O'Neil from Kalispell. For this trip I had learned how to write in advance to the park headquarters and give the names of the anticipated people and a few details like where they were from to guarantee us beds in the dorms. In due time, I was informed that we were successfully scheduled in and official plans were made.

I took our sedan and Ivan took his vehicle to accommodate the seven of us. It was a beautiful time of year and we got to see the beauty of the fall colors, especially on the aspen trees. As usual, I wasn't very flush with money, but I did the best I could to help the others in the family enjoy this wonderful hike. It certainly isn't a wilderness experience with wall-to-wall hikers coming and going, but the north rim was still beautiful with all the foliage around. Looking down at the canyon where the trail zig-zags, you wonder how you're going to find a way down, but it manages to loop back and forth. We enjoyed the trail and the ever-changing canyons that we passed through on our way down.

From left: Ivan, Andy, Bette, Bobbi, John, Bill, and me

For the first day I thought I would enjoy a nice lunch and I had even boiled an egg at the cabin on the north rim the night before as a special treat for my lunch. However, I was afraid I wasn't going to have room in my backpack to carry everything and I asked Bette if she could carry my lunch, which she agreed to. But woe is me, when we were loading our packs in the back of the car at the trailhead I failed to give her my lunch so that it could be packed. I thought she would take it, but she didn't. As I was thinking about my wonderful lunch on the hike I thought, oh lord mercy, I need that lunch! It was a strenuous hike and I'm a person that needs food regularly. When the time came we walked off the trail to an inviting little creek, and of course, my lunch was nowhere in sight.

When I mentioned that I didn't have a lunch, Bill said, "I'll give you half of my sandwich, Dad" and that was a blessing I gladly accepted. Why I didn't have additional snacks I don't know, but Bill saved the day.

Another thing that turned out to be a real problem was that I had not taken any thinner socks, but had relied on advice of others who said to have thick socks to avoid blisters. But my beloved Danner light-weight hiking boots were too small for thick socks, so that didn't match up well. How dumb can you get? I toughed it out for quite a ways, but my feet were hurting about two thirds of the way so I had to take off my boots and wear my little low-cut tennis shoes. These weren't designed to support someone with a load, but that was my only alternative.

Ivan was the leader of our group and he set a fair pace. A month shy from 69 years old, I was always the last one in line, but in one instance Bobbi was behind me instead with the rest of our group was up ahead. The Kaibab was also the mule trail and the mules were

Ivan O'Neil at the entrance to the Phantom Ranch

stopped once and a while so the dudes could stretch their legs and the mules could take a break on the trail. Our main group had pressed ahead of the mule rest stop and Bobbi and I were lagging a little. It was at a bend in the trail and we had just gotten around most of the mules when the last mule deliberately turned and swung his rump around to block the trail. Not wanting to be left further behind by our group, I took a chance on trying to sneak by the mule on the outside edge of the trail. I had read a book on the Grand Canyon that said the mules were well-trained and gentle, and I grabbed on to the sides of the saddle. Down below about fifteen feet was the ravine and I swung around the mule, not saying anything

to Bobbi, and she did the same thing as I did. But we were virtually hanging over the edge. We were lucky to make it by. I think it gave us both kind of a scare. But we did what we had to and got by thanks to the well-trained mules, even though one was being a pest.

It's a little odd, but for some reason we didn't mention our little scare until Bobbi was reading the draft of this manuscript very recently. She said that when she grabbed the saddle of the mule, the mule showed its displeasure by swatting her in the face with its tail. Fortunately it didn't cause Bobbi to loosen her grip on the saddle, and she swung past the mule and we both hurried on to join our group. Bobbi never followed

Bobbi and me at Ribbon Falls

behind me after that. Smart girl. The rest of the trail was mostly downhill, which was greatly appreciated, but it was going to be about all I could handle.

I was a slow hiker anyway, so I was usually last in the line of our group and was hoping I could make it all in time for our reservation at the mess hall at the Phantom Ranch. I was getting weary, and my feet were hurting, but we came to an optional one-mile side journey to Ribbon Falls when we were fairly close to the Phantom Ranch.

I decided to join the others and take this hike, but it was hot and tiring at that time. When we finally made to the waterfall, it was kind of like a paradise, as it was cool under the cliff and the nearby falls was just a ribbon of water spraying down from above. The immediate area had lots of moss and ferns and certainly a welcome rest stop, but we knew we couldn't linger too long because the time was passing and we had the deadline to get to our supper reservations. As usual, I was the last one to drag in. It would have been fun if we all could have eaten supper together, but there was only seating for five of us in our group so the youngest got to eat first and Ivan and I ate less than an hour later on the next shift. When I made reservations for the meals they not only included the supper, but breakfast for all of us. Plus we had opted to have them prepare a sack lunch for that hike out on the Bright Angel Trail. So my lunch was taken care of for that day, and this time I made sure it was packed!

Back in Missoula, I gradually lost contact with friends of the past as time went on. Clark, who had accompanied me on the Mexico trip, had gone back to his family's wheat ranch and was married and they had three girls. We visited him occasionally and he was able to accompany us on a few hikes, but it was pretty seldom. It was a similar situation with my crew from the war. Charlie was in California, which was too far away to visit, but one I especially hated losing touch with was Hanwell, our radio operator. He wrote to me and said that he was going to change his last name to that of his stepfather. He was also going to move from Detroit to Canada perhaps, and I never wrote his new name or address down or kept track of him. I did have some contact with Roy Walser, our co-pilot, because he had moved to Spokane, only a few hours away. He also had a sister that moved to Hamilton in the realty business. So a few times over the years we were in touch with each other. To this date Roy is still living in Mesa, Arizona.

Thanks to the 8th Air Force Historical Society I was also able to go to a few reunions held at different cities throughout the country each year and meet with the 493rd Group veterans and their spouses. Whole groups come together and it was and still is quite an occasion each year. The tail gunner of our crew, Peck Owens, and I met at such a reunion around 1994. He said he owed his life to me because I brought him back. I told him that I wanted to get back just as much as he did and that we had all had to work as a team, but he credited me as the pilot. He was in the sporting goods business with his dad and then later on his own. After we got reacquainted he sent me several gifts of clothing that he had access to in the sporting world, and he had them printed up with our group insignia and name on it. Later, at another reunion, he told me that when group operations were looking for a temporary replacement tail-gunner for a mission they would come by and ask him if he would be willing to go on a mission with another crew. He said he wouldn't fly with anybody but me. It was a nice loyal gesture, but I couldn't have given

Unofficial patch designed by the late Bill Overbeck showing the years we were in Debach as well as the B-17 above and the B-24 below

any guarantees on safety, none of us could have. I attended several of these reunions, but it was expensive and later a little hard to attend. Me, my friend Jack, and Peck would go to afew of them together, but Peck had health problems and had had real extensive surgery when he was still in Texas with his sporting goods business. He had urinary and colon surgeries, so it was pretty serious. One time he got an infection just about the time we were going to meet at a reunion and he couldn't make it. But we did manage several reunions all together.

Now, at age 93, Shirl and I stick pretty close to home, but we are lucky to be as good as we are health-wise. We lived in our house at 2428 Agnes for 24 years until we were surrounded by noisy commercial activities, so in October 1979 we moved to the northern outskirts of Missoula. There we found a home that really appealed to us in the Lincolnwood addition of the Rattlesnake Valley. We hadn't sold our house yet, but it was so right for the both of us. It had a good sized lot with a variety of trees, plus a small seasonal creek with swift running water. The lawn was covered with bright yellow cottonwood leaves, plus the house was built low to the ground with easy access for a wheelchair through the garage. Now, 36 years later, I'm still thankful to be living here. We have a beautiful unobstructed view of Mt. Jumbo with the changing seasons thanks to wide fields and a winery to the east of us. A number of graceful white-tailed deer travel through our yard to the field every year.

We have some very nice neighbors who are very supportive as we have aged. Our neighbors Ray and Delores Wiegert, who live across the street, are exceptionally helpful and kind, going above and beyond the call of duty by picking up our mail each day and bringing it to us from the mailbox down the street and getting our garbage out early in the morning on pickup day. There is only a limited period we can have our garbage out because of troubles with bears looking for a free meal. Not only that, but Ray has shoveled the snow off of our sidewalk and driveway for many years now despite his own age, as he is a retired minister with 55 years of service.

From our home in Lincolnwood we got to watch our family expand. We are so lucky that our youngest daughter Bobbi and her husband John Combs, the former Hellgate High School band director, moved less than a mile away from our home. We've been blessed to be able to watch their three daughters Amanda, Lindsay, and Elena, grow and change from babies into young adult women. Our lives were enriched by the concerts and music events that we were able to attend and enjoy while these three grandchildren were in the music program. We so enjoyed watching their performances.

Our son Bill married Sue O'Neil of Kalispell and they also had three children, April, Andy, and Marisa, and resided in Kalispell. Shirl and I are also now the proud great-grandparents of Rylee and Alia, April's children, Eliana and Liam, Andy and Lucy's children, and baby Marian, Marisa and Matt Hoyne's daughter.

Bette and her husband Greg Clark live five miles west of Plains, Montana and have a tree farm. Bette comes to Missoula as often as she can to help with shopping and doctor appointments, etc. She often stays overnight.

My friend Jack copied my brother's diaries on his computer and later I decided to

Jack with a store-front character on an adventure of ours in South Dakota

223

publish a book on my brother's life with heavy emphasis on his time in Missoula and his service in World War II as a P-38 fighter pilot with the 12th Air Force. Over an extended time, with Jack's encouragement, I finally completed it. The book is still available through Pictorial Histories in Missoula. Bill wrote in detail about flying and the problems that he faced alone as a fighter pilot, and a large part of his book was based on his diaries. The reason I kept my own diaries were because of his influence. Bill's name is also listed on the World War II Memorial in Rose Park in Missoula.

Here I had published Bill's book, but now I reflected on my own life. I also wanted to have my say as seen through the eyes of a bomber pilot and express my feelings to add to the knowledge of one who was severely impacted by the war and how much fate seems to play in your life. Another B-24 pilot from Missoula comes to mind. Guy Rogers, a little older than me, went over to Germany ahead of me. On their first mission over Berlin on March 1st, 1944 they were shot down and he was one of the few that survived after bailing out. He was taken prisoner and he had a severe injury, losing a leg. All on his first mission. That's why war is such a hell and it is a total waste of life.

But I am proud to say that I flew with the 8th Air Force and never aborted a combat mission. My brother Bill was so proud of me and it was a tragedy that he had to lose his life just as so many young men did. He never knew that I had followed in his footsteps flying a B-24 bomber over to England. Wouldn't it have been neat to have him fly his P-38 to our 493rd bomb group base at Debach, England? I could then have introduced him to my crew and we could have had a mutual admiration celebration, he was so proud of me and I was so proud of him. So much for that dream. Our crew was lucky to survive. Thank you, Lord!

My life after the war was a lot stormier than it should have been because of some dumb decisions I made, but I have much to be thankful for. Shirl heads the list, and with her I have enjoyed a wonderful family in our life together. Polio was a dreadful blow, but she survived and made the best of it. We are fortunate to have had 67 years together. Old age is taking its toll, but we have endured together. So we're luckier than most.

Shirl and me in 2005

In our home in Lincolnwood - 2015

34068172R00140

Made in the USA
San Bernardino, CA
17 May 2016